Computer Monographs

GENERAL EDITOR: Stanley Gill, M.A., Ph.D.
ASSOCIATE EDITOR: J. J. Florentin, Ph.D., Imperial College, London

The Programmer's Introduction to LISP

For David,
my son

The Programmer's Introduction to LISP

W. D. Maurer

Assistant Professor, Department of
Electrical Engineering and Computer Sciences,
University of California,
Berkeley, California

Macdonald · London and
American Elsevier Inc. · New York

© W. D. Maurer 1972

Sole distributors for the British Isles and Commonwealth
Macdonald & Co. (Publishers) Ltd.
49–50 Poland Street, London W.1

Sole distributors for the United States and Dependencies
American Elsevier Publishing Company Inc.
52 Vanderbilt Avenue, New York, N.Y. 10017

All remaining areas
Elsevier Publishing Company
P.O. Box 211, Jan van Galenstraat 335, Amsterdam, The Netherlands

Macdonald SBN 356 03980 3
American Elsevier ISBN 0 444 19572 6
Library of Congress Catalog Card No 79 185637

All Rights Reserved. No part of this publication may be reproduced, stored in a retrieval system, or transmitted, in any form or by any means, electronic, mechanical, photocopying, recording or otherwise, without prior permission of the publishers.

Made and printed in Great Britain by
Hazell Watson & Viney Ltd., Aylesbury, Bucks

Contents

	Page
Preface	vii
1 Standard Functions	1
1.1 Arithmetic expressions	1
1.2 S-expressions	3
1.3 Atoms	5
1.4 Symbolic data	6
1.5 Lists	8
1.6 Sublists	10
1.7 Recursion	11
1.8 Using a LISP system	13
1.9 Using subexpressions	15
Exercises	17
2 Constructing Functions	22
2.1 LISP functions	22
2.2 Mathematical logic in LISP	24
2.3 Parameters	26
2.4 List-processing functions	28
2.5 Predicate functions	30
2.6 Conditionals	31
2.7 Recursive functions	33
2.8 Recursive list processing	35
2.9 Sublists and recursion	37
2.10 Recursive predicates	39
2.11 Logical operators	40
2.12 Dot notation	42
2.13 Recursive functions of two lists	45

CONTENTS

    2.14 Type functions   47
             Exercises   49

3 Constructing Programs   57

    3.1   LISP programs   57
    3.2   List processing programs   59
    3.3   Constructing lists   61
    3.4   The effect of a function   63
    3.5   Predicates written as programs   65
    3.6   Recursive programs   67
    3.7   Grouping functions   69
    3.8   The evaluation rule   71
    3.9   The evaluation function   73
    3.10 Programs as data   75
    3.11 Input-output   78
           Exercises   81

4 Further Topics   86

    4.1   Further arithmetic functions   86
    4.2   Function definitions in programs   87
    4.3   Compiling   89
    4.4   Machine-dependent features of LISP   91
    4.5   Garbage collection   93
    4.6   Miscellaneous topics   95
           Exercises   98

References   100

Answers to starred exercises   102

Index   109

Preface

LISP is a programming language developed by John McCarthy and his students while he was on the faculty of the Massachusetts Institute of Technology. Many of his students made important contributions; in particular, it was Daniel Edwards who programmed the garbage collection process.

At the time LISP was developed (*circa* 1960), it was not common for college and university students to learn computer programming in any language unless they intended to become computer professionals. Partly because of this, the first textbooks on LISP did not assume that the student knew any other programming language. It was, in fact, found possible to teach LISP as the student's first language if he had sufficient mathematical maturity.

Today, partly because of the lower cost of computers and the increased speed of compilers, and partly because of time-sharing – a field in whose development John McCarthy also played a critical part – almost all engineering students and most science students learn an algebraic language in college, normally FORTRAN, ALGOL, BASIC, or PL/1. This book is designed for the needs of these students. It is hoped that learning LISP will alert at least some students to the delights of mathematical logic; for all who are seriously interested in computer programming, however, list processing is a fundamental subject, and LISP is the best-known language which was designed for list processing.

LISP is not an algebraic language (although MLISP, which is not studied in this book, is algebraic). LISP may be characterized as a functional language, as a symbolic language, as a list processing language, as a recursive language, and as a logical language. All of these facets of LISP are studied and brought together in this book.

PREFACE

Unlike some other books on programming, this book is designed primarily for classroom use rather than for self-teaching, although it may profitably be used in either way. In line with this philosophy, the answers to some of the exercises, but not all, may be found at the end of the book.

All good programming languages have dialects, and LISP is no exception. The student who wishes to learn about principles of a large number of LISP systems would do well to read the entire book. However, difficulties may arise when he attempts to run some practice problems on an actual computer and discovers that the LISP system which is available to him does not have all the features which are discussed here. It is the instructor's prerogative to compare the facilities of his LISP system with those described here, and to point out to the students where the discrepancies are. The more conscientious instructor may supervise advanced student projects to modify an existing LISP system so that it acquires more such features.

This book has been used in an advanced programming course at the University of California at Berkeley, attended by both undergraduate and graduate students. The author would like to extend special thanks to Dr James Griesmer of IBM for testing the functions and programs in this book on the LISP 1.14 system operating under the CP/CMS time-sharing system at the Watson Research Center in Yorktown Heights, New York; and to Peter Deutsch, John Miller and Larry Tesler, who read the manuscript thoroughly and suggested many valuable modifications.

Berkeley, California, 1971   W. D. Maurer

1 Standard functions

1.1 Arithmetic expressions

LISP is a *functional* language. This means that every type of construction which may be performed in LISP, and which is a function in the mathematical sense, is implemented in LISP as a function.

Functions are quite common in programming languages. If we wish to use the mathematical expression sin x, for example, we may write SIN(X) in either FORTRAN or ALGOL. In LISP we would write

>   (SIN X)

(or sometimes SIN(X)). But in FORTRAN or ALGOL if we wish to form the sum of two numbers X and Y we would write X + Y. In LISP it would be

>   (PLUS X Y)

This is because of the fact that when we write the symbol + between two constants or variables in FORTRAN or ALGOL, we are implicitly using a function of two variables. We could, if we wanted to, write FUNCTION PLUS (X, Y) in FORTRAN, or **procedure** plus (x, y); in ALGOL, but we normally do not, because FORTRAN and ALGOL are *algebraic* languages, in which the four commonest functions – addition, subtraction, multiplication, and division – are handled in special ways.

It is also quite common, in various programming languages, to be able to use functions inside other functions. If we needed the sine of the sine of x in FORTRAN or ALGOL, we could write SIN (SIN(X)). In LISP, in a similar way, we could write

>   (SIN (SIN X))

Similarly with the PLUS function we could write

(PLUS X (PLUS Y Z))

If this were written in FORTRAN or ALGOL as **PLUS(X, PLUS(Y, Z))**, where **PLUS(X, Y)** had been defined as $X + Y$, the result would, of course, be $X + Y + Z$. If we define the LISP function

(TIMES X Y)

to be $X * Y$, then the expressions

(PLUS X (TIMES Y Z))

and

(PLUS (TIMES X Y) Z)

stand for $X + Y * Z$ and $X * Y + Z$, respectively.

It is clear that we can express, in this way, any arithmetic expression involving the operators + and *. This includes parenthesized expressions; if we wish to use $(A + B) * (C + D)$, for example, we would write

(TIMES (PLUS A B) (PLUS C D))

in LISP. Also, if a large number of quantities are to be added or multiplied together, we may express all of these quantities as arguments to the PLUS or TIMES function. Thus the expression

(PLUS X Y Z)

has the same effect as **(PLUS X (PLUS Y Z))**.

There are two different MINUS functions in LISP, one called MINUS and one called DIFFERENCE. The DIFFERENCE function is analogous to ordinary subtraction; thus

(DIFFERENCE X Y)

gives the result $X - Y$. The MINUS function is analogous to the so-called *unary minus*, or the use of the minus sign to denote the negative of a quantity; thus

(MINUS X)

gives $-X$ as its result. Notice that DIFFERENCE always has two arguments, and MINUS always has one. The QUOTIENT function

STANDARD FUNCTIONS

is analogous to the DIFFERENCE function; thus the expression

(QUOTIENT X Y)

has as its result X/Y. There is also a REMAINDER function; thus

(REMAINDER X Y)

has as its value the remainder when X is divided by Y.

1.2 S-expressions

The use of functions in LISP has both an advantage and a disadvantage. The disadvantage, of course, is that the resulting expressions are lengthier and have more parentheses. It is certainly easier to write $\frac{-b + \sqrt{(b^2 - 4ac)}}{2a}$ – or even (−B + SQRT(B * B − 4 * A * C))/ (2 *A) – than it is to write

(QUOTIENT (PLUS (MINUS B) (SQRT (DIFFERENCE (TIMES B B) (TIMES 4 A C)))) (TIMES 2 A))

Because of this, many LISP systems have special facilities* for writing arithmetic expressions in the usual way. Here, however, we shall not learn about these facilities. The reason is that we are going to learn how to use LISP for a wide variety of other functions than the special ones of addition, subtraction, multiplication, and division. Most of the time, we will in fact be using LISP for other purposes than those of algebraic functions.

The advantage of LISP's functional notation is that it unifies LISP in much the same way that the notions of set and function unify mathematics. There is, in fact, only one kind of construction to learn in LISP, and that is the function. Every other feature of LISP, such as defining functions, conditionals, transfer of control in a program, and so on, is defined in LISP by creating a special function to handle it.

Expressions in LISP such as the ones we have been writing are known as *S-expressions*. There are only two types of constituents in an S-expression: the 'elements' such as X and 2, which we call *atoms*,

* See, for example, the MLISP manual, cited in the references at the end of this book.

3

THE PROGRAMMER'S INTRODUCTION TO LISP

and the parentheses. It is clear, however, that not every expression which contains atoms and parentheses is an S-expression. Thus the four constructions

>   (PLUS X (PLUS Y Z)
>   (DIFFERENCE R S)))
>   )PLUS X)PLUS Y Z((
>   (PLUS 4 2))(PLUS (PLUS 5 6)

are not properly formed. The first two are not S-expressions because their parentheses do not balance; in the first one, there are too many left parentheses, while in the second, there are too many right parentheses. The third construction starts with a right parenthesis, and so, even though the parentheses balance, it is illegal. The mistake in the last construction above, however, is not so easy to pinpoint. It has three left parentheses and three right parentheses, and yet it is clearly meaningless. If we look at the characters

>   (PLUS 4 2)

at the beginning of this construction, we can see that they form an S-expression in themselves; this is followed by a right parenthesis, and the result is therefore illegal. Based on this observation we may define an S-expression as follows: *an S-expression is made up of atoms (which may be constants or variables) and parentheses in such a way that if we imagine a counter set to zero, increased by one for each left parenthesis encountered in order from left to right, and decreased by one for each right parenthesis so encountered, then the counter has final value zero, and is always strictly positive except at the beginning and the end.* Thus in the last of the four constructions above, the counter first assumes the value 1 upon passing the first left parenthesis; then 0, upon passing the first right parenthesis; and then -1, because there is another right parenthesis immediately following. Since it does not remain positive, let alone strictly positive, the given construction is not properly formed.

In Section 1.7 we shall introduce another definition of an S-expression, which is much less cumbersome than this one. Meanwhile, we must mention one other very important character in an S-expression: the blank. In FORTRAN and in many versions of ALGOL, blanks are ignored; but in LISP, this is decidedly not the case. A

STANDARD FUNCTIONS

blank is used, when necessary, to separate arguments. LISP does provide that a comma can be used instead; thus

  (PLUS X Y) (PLUS X,Y)
  (PLUS,X Y) (PLUS,X,Y)

are equivalent representations of $X + Y$. In practice, however, there are very few LISP programmers who actually use commas. As usual in programming languages, a string of blanks may always be used instead of a single blank. The blank may be left out, if desired, before or after a left or right parenthesis; thus

  (TIMES(PLUS A B)C(PLUS D E)(PLUS F G))

and

  (TIMES (PLUS A B) C (PLUS D E) (PLUS F G))

are both legal and are equivalent to each other.

1.3 Atoms

The constants and the variables in an S-expression, as we have seen, are called atoms. In the modern world, in which we study the components of an atom (in physics) such as electrons, protons, and neutrons, it is easy to forget that the original meaning of the word 'atom' is *that which cannot be divided further,* and this is the sense in which 'atom' is used in LISP. (The Greek roots are *a*, not, and *tom-*, part; *tom-* also means 'volume', that is a *part* of a large book.)

Variables follow the usual rules for an identifier. A variable name must start with a letter and must be composed of letters and numbers only. There is one major difference: whereas, in other languages there is usually an upper limit on the number of characters which may be contained in an atom, in most LISP systems there is none. *Any* string of letters and numbers, starting with a letter, may serve as the name of an atom, and may be treated as a variable.

There are certain special identifiers which are *reserved* in LISP. The concept of a reserved word may be new to those who know no other languages than FORTRAN and ALGOL. In FORTRAN, if we want to use a variable called IF, or DO, or CALL, there is nothing to prevent us from doing so; in ALGOL, the key words are enclosed in quotes, and so there is no confusion, for example, between 'BEGIN' and BEGIN. In many other languages, however, particularly COBOL, there is a list of special words which cannot be used as variable names. In LISP, the rule is not very clear-cut. Most LISP systems will allow you to use one of the special words as a variable, but warn you that unpredictable consequences may occur. In particular, the identifiers T, F, and NIL should not be used as variable names. T and F mean 'true' and 'false', respectively, and serve much the same function as the FORTRAN .TRUE. and .FALSE. or the ALGOL **true** and **false**. NIL has a number of uses, one of which is as a substitute for F; in fact, F is not used very much to mean 'false', and NIL is used instead.

Constants follow various rules in various LISP systems. Most LISP systems will recognize both integers and floating point constants. Integers may sometimes be given in octal or binary as well as decimal.

A variable may have a *value* in LISP, just as in FORTRAN or ALGOL. One way to give a variable a value is to use the function SETQ, which acts somewhat like an assignment statement. Writing

(SETQ X 5)

will set X to 5; that is, it will be like the FORTRAN statement X = 5 or the ALGOL statement X:= 5;. The first argument is the variable to be set; the second argument, the quantity which is placed there. As usual, this second argument may be as involved as necessary. Thus

(SETQ X (PLUS Y 1))

sets X to $Y + 1$; it is analogous to X = Y + 1 in FORTRAN.

1.4 Symbolic data

Besides being a functional language, LISP is a *symbolic* language. One of the most important features of LISP is that the data which it manipulates is not necessarily composed of numbers.

As a relatively simple example of this, we can set the value of a variable, such as X, to be another atom, such as Y. Note that this is

STANDARD FUNCTIONS

quite different from 'setting X to Y' in the usual sense; thus the function

(SETQ X Y)

would set X to the *value* of Y; if Y had been set equal to 4, then **(SETQ X Y)** would set X equal to 4. Notice that this works both ways; if Y had been set equal to Z (the symbol, not the thing that Z stands for) then **(SETQ X Y)** would set X equal to Z.

To set symbols equal to other symbols in the first place, we may use the QUOTE function. Thus

(SETQ X (QUOTE Y))

sets X equal to the symbol Y. A short explanation of this is in order. QUOTE is a function whose value is its argument; thus the value of **(QUOTE Y)** is Y. We now begin to see a certain consistency in LISP: just as **(SETQ X Y)** set X to the value of Y, **(SETQ X (QUOTE Y))** sets X to the value of **(QUOTE Y)** – which is Y.

As a further example of this, we may consider the function SET. The expression **(SET (QUOTE X) Y)** is equivalent to **(SETQ X Y)**. The expression **(SET X Y)** sets the *value* of X to the value of Y. Note that this makes no sense if X and Y have ordinary numeric values. If X is 3 and Y is 6, **(SET X Y)** would set 3 to 6, which is ridiculous. But if the value of X is the symbol Z, **(SET X Y)** sets Z to the value of Y.

The internal consistency of LISP goes even further. *Every* atom in LISP has a value. Each number which appears in a LISP program is an atom; the value of this atom is itself. This is an important characteristic of numbers in LISP which is usually *not* true of symbolic atoms. Thus if we write

(SETQ P 3)

we are setting P to the value of 3, which is 3. If we write

(SETQ P Q)

on the other hand, we are setting P to the value of Q, which is usually not (the symbol) Q itself.

The value of T, the special atom meaning 'true', is T itself. The value of F (for 'false') is NIL, and the value of NIL is NIL. These conventions are partly historical in nature, and partly they have to do

7

THE PROGRAMMER'S INTRODUCTION TO LISP

with the internal workings of certain LISP systems. On certain older LISP systems, the value of T is another special atom, $*T*$, and the value of $*T*$ is $*T*$.

If the value of an atom is another atom with a symbolic name, the numerical functions will give meaningless results. It clearly makes no sense to say **(PLUS X Y)** if the value of Y is the symbol Z. Later we shall study some functions which apply to symbolic data.

1.5 Lists

Another type of data in LISP is the *list*. Besides being a functional language and a symbolic language, LISP is a *list processing* language as well.

On the surface, a list in LISP is somewhat similar to an array in FORTRAN or ALGOL. It is an ordered collection of data; thus

(1 2 9 P 7 THETA 2.9)

is the S-expression of a list of seven elements. However, here the resemblance ends. In the first place, a list cannot be 'indexed' in the way that an array can. If we wish to refer to the sixth item in this list – in this case, THETA – we cannot simply put the number 6 in an index register or its equivalent and expect to be able to fetch the atom THETA immediately. This is because of the way in which atoms on a list, or references to them, are 'chained' together: each reference has associated with it a pointer to the next reference. This means that the addresses of the various atom references are not in sequence, the way they would be in an array.

If we tried to write

(SETQ X (1 2 9 P 7 THETA 2.9))

to set the value of X to the list above, we would run into a problem. To see it, note that earlier we treated the use of

(SETQ X (PLUS Y 1))

to set X to the value of Y plus one. We do not want this to set X to the list of three elements PLUS, Y, and 1. In order to do this, we make a convention: whenever an expression (such as **(PLUS Y 1)**) occurs inside an S-expression, the *first* atom encountered (in this

STANDARD FUNCTIONS

case it is PLUS) is taken to specify a function. The remaining atoms are taken to be the arguments of the function. Of course, some of these may not really be atoms; we might have said

(SETQ X (PLUS Y (TIMES Z 4)))

which includes (TIMES Z 4) as an argument of the PLUS function – but if this happens, the same rule is applied again; the first atom occurring in this subexpression, namely TIMES, is taken to be a function with Z and 4 as its arguments.

We can now see why (SETQ X (1 2 9 P 7 THETA 2.9)) would not work. In this case, the first atom in the subexpression is 1, and 1 would be taken to be the name of a function! Since there is no function in LISP called 1, the system would report an error.

To remedy this unfortunate state of affairs, we could write

(SETQ X (QUOTE (1 2 9 P 7 THETA 2.9)))

The value of (QUOTE (1 2 9 P 7 THETA 2.9)) is (1 2 9 P 7 THETA 2·9). In the QUOTE function, and *only* in the QUOTE function, the general rule mentioned above is not followed. Thus the number 1 is not taken here to be the name of a function, and the value of the QUOTE function in this case, as in any case, is the argument of the QUOTE function, just as it stands.

There is another way of producing a list as the value of a function. The function LIST produces as its value a list of its arguments. Thus the value of

(LIST 1 9 4 6 3)

is (1 9 4 6 3). This is, of course, the same as the value of

(QUOTE (1 9 4 6 3))

However, when the arguments, for example, are symbolic, there is a difference between LIST with several arguments and QUOTE applied to a list of these arguments. If X has been set to 2, then (LIST 1 X 3 X) has the value (1 2 3 2), whereas (QUOTE (1 X 3 X)) has the value (1 X 3 X).

Any function can have, as its value, a list. In particular, there is one arithmetic function, called DIVIDE, which has as its value a list of two atoms – the quotient and the remainder. Thus

(DIVIDE 65 3)

P.I.L.—2

has the value (21 2). Such a list, however, cannot be used directly by the arithmetic functions, even if it consists of only one element. Thus, for example, (PLUS X 4) is meaningless (and will cause an error) if X is the list (3), although it is equal to 7 if X is the atom 3.

1.6 Sublists

Because of the way in which the elements of a list are chained together in memory, it is possible for them to be either atoms or *sublists*. A sublist is simply a list which is contained within another list. For example, we might want to make a list of four items, 6, 7, 9, and X, where X stands for another list of three items, 10, 11, and 14. In this case, we would write

(6 7 9 (10 11 14))

as the S-expression for this list.

The sublists of a list may have sublists, and so an *ad infinitum*. Thus

((1 6) 7 ((8 4) 3))

is a list of three elements. The first of these is a list of two elements, 1 and 6. The second is an atom, namely 7. The third is a list of two elements, of which the second is the atom 3, while the first is a list of the two elements 8 and 4.

We can now see the relation between LISP as a list processing language and as a functional language. The function expressions, or S-expressions, which specify function calls in LISP, also specify lists. Thus

(SETQ X (PLUS Y (TIMES Z 4)))

is a list of three elements. The first is SETQ, the second is X, and the third is itself a list of three elements. On this list, the first element is PLUS, the second is Y, and the third is a list of the three elements TIMES, Z, and 4.

In fact, *a function reference in LISP appears in memory as a list.* This means that whenever an S-expression such as (PLUS X Y) occurs anywhere within a LISP program that has been read into memory, a list is formed – in this case, a list of three elements,

PLUS, X, and Y. The first element of such a list will normally be an atom, as it stands for a function – although there are some cases in which a sublist can be used in this position as well, to specify a function. The remaining elements of the list are the arguments, and they are either atoms or sublists. A sublist in this position specifies a function inside the original function. We say that the given function reference is *represented* as a list (in memory).

As a general rule, we may say that *to every S-expression in LISP there corresponds a list, and to every list in LISP there corresponds an S-expression.* The second part of this statement has been slightly relaxed in many LISP systems; there are special functions which can form a list that does not have an S-expression. For the present, however, we shall confine ourselves to lists which have S-expressions.

1.7 Recursion

Besides being a functional language, a symbolic language, and a list processing language, LISP is a *recursive* language. This statement, however, means much more in LISP than it does in ALGOL. In ALGOL we can have functions which call themselves, either directly or indirectly. If the function A contains a call to itself, then we say that it calls itself directly. If the function A calls B and the function B calls A, then we say that A calls itself indirectly. More generally, if there are several functions, $A_1, A_2, \ldots, A_n$, such that A_i calls A_{i+1} for $1 \leq i < n$, and A_n calls A_1, then we say that A_1 calls itself indirectly (and, for that matter, so do all the other A_i). In FORTRAN, of course, none of this is possible. We say that ALGOL *allows functions to be recursive,* whereas FORTRAN does not.

In LISP, when we define a function, this function can, in fact, be recursive, just as in ALGOL. But in LISP we also use the concept of recursive function as it is defined in logic.

When we define the factorial of n to be n multiplied by the factorial of $n - 1$, we are making a *circular* definition. We are defining the word 'factorial' by using a definition which includes the word 'factorial' itself. Ordinarily, this would make the definition improper; but if we specify that the factorial of 0 is 1, the definition does, in fact, give the value of the factorial of any positive integer. In particular, the factorial of 1 is 1 times the factorial of 0, that is 1. The factorial of 2 is 2 times the factorial of 1, that is 2. In this way we can determine from the definition above the factorial of 2, 3, et cetera, in order. Definitions such as the above, which appear to be circular but in fact specify a function uniquely over a certain range, are called definitions of *recursive functions*.

Many functions have recursive definitions in addition to their ordinary definitions. For example, we might define multiplication $x \cdot y$ by the specification $x \cdot y = x + (x \cdot (y - 1))$, where $x \cdot 0 = 0$. This definition specifies $x \cdot y$ for all positive integers y, although it does not work for negative integers or for real numbers which are not integers. Another example of this is the definition, in ALGOL, of an unsigned integer as either a digit or a digit followed by an unsigned integer. This is the same as specifying an unsigned integer to be a sequence of digits, of arbitrary length ≥ 1.

We are now in a position to make a new definition of an S-expression, as promised in Section 1.2. This definition, which is recursive, is as follows: <u>an S-expression is either an atom, or it is a left parenthesis followed by a sequence of S-expressions separated by blanks or commas and followed by a right parenthesis.</u> The S-expressions in the sequence may themselves, of course, be atoms or further sequences. Thus, for example,

((1 6) 7 ((8 4) 3))

consists of a left parenthesis, followed by the sequence of S-expressions (1 6), 7, and ((8 4) 3), followed by a right parenthesis. Each of these expressions may be determined to be an S-expression in the same way.

Similarly, *a list is a sequence of references, each one of which may refer to an atom or a list*. In connection with this recursive definition, it is important to note that a list is *not* a sequence of atoms. The distinction is a fine one, but important. An atom is represented in memory by an item which includes its name and which may also include various properties of the atom. A list which 'includes' this atom includes only a *pointer* to the atom. Thus a list, in LISP, is a list of pairs; one member of each pair is a pointer to an atom or a pointer to a sublist, while the other member is a pointer to the next pair. This organization of memory is very easy to implement on the IBM 700 series of computers, which were the first to have a LISP system, because on these computers each 36-bit word has two special 15-bit fields,

STANDARD FUNCTIONS

the *address* and *decrement* fields, each of which may be referenced separately, and each of which is just large enough to contain a pointer.

1.8 Using a LISP system

At this point we may collect what we know about LISP and try out some actual S-expressions on a computer. It is true that we still have not discussed how to write a function or a program in LISP. However, most LISP systems have a facility which allows us to make some preliminary experimentation without worrying about functions or programs at all, other than the standard functions which are defined by the LISP system in much the same way as the standard functions SIN, COS, etc., are defined in a FORTRAN or ALGOL system.

The operation of a LISP system is quite different from that of most ALGOL or FORTRAN systems. In FORTRAN we normally speak of the FORTRAN *compiler*: the source program goes in, an object program comes out, and then the object program is executed. In LISP, the normal operation is under the control of an *interpreter*. A function is entered into the system; its value is calculated and printed; then another function is entered, and so on. (Compilers for LISP also exist; see Section 4.3.)

Some LISP systems work on time-sharing computers, in which each user has a teletype terminal or its equivalent. In this case, the input lines to LISP are typed. Other LISP systems work on batch-processing computers which read cards, either directly or indirectly, and in such a case an input line to LISP is given on one or more cards. In what follows we shall refer simply to *input lines*, which may be thought of either as having been typed or as having been keypunched on cards and the cards presented to the computer.

If the LISP system reads the input line

PLUS (3 5)

it prints out 8. A word of explanation is in order here. In Section 1.1 we mentioned that the expression **(SIN X)** is sometimes written **SIN(X)**. Similarly, **(PLUS X Y)** is sometimes written as **PLUS (X Y)**. We shall now discuss what we mean by 'sometimes'.

For mainly historical reasons, the LISP system*, when it is reading

* On certain LISP systems, the rest of this chapter may be ignored.

13

functions to be evaluated, reads not one S-expression but *two* at a time. The first S-expression specifies a function; the second, a list of its arguments. Thus when the LISP system reads **PLUS (X Y)**, it is actually reading the S-expression **PLUS** followed by the S-expression **(X Y)**. It is easy to think of **PLUS (X Y)** as having been derived from **(PLUS X Y)** by moving the first left parenthesis forward, so that it appears after the first element of the S-expression instead of before it. However, this 'short cut' fails when we consider sublists of the list that gives the S-expression. If we were to write

PLUS (3 PLUS (5 7))

as an input line to the LISP system, meaning 3 + (5 + 7) or 15, the system would signal an error, because the list **(3 PLUS (5 7))** is a list of *three* quantities – the integer 3, the symbol PLUS, and the list (5 7). Thus the form **PLUS (5 7)** cannot be used inside another pair of parentheses.

The 'short cut', however, is widely used, with the following modification: whenever we use a function at the *top level* (not enclosed by any parentheses), we use a form like **PLUS (X Y)**. Whenever we use a function *not* at the top level, we use a form like **(PLUS X Y)**. The phrase 'top level' as used above is a special case of the concept of *parenthesis level*. Any atom within an S-expression is at some parenthesis level, which is, in fact, the value of the counter mentioned in the earlier definition of an S-expression which was given in Section 1.2. To find the parenthesis level of an atom, we count the left and right parentheses to the *left* of that atom, and subtract the second from the first. Thus in

((1 6) 7 ((8 4) 3))

the atom 8 has parenthesis level 3. The top level then corresponds to parenthesis level zero.

Any of the LISP functions which we have introduced may now be tried out at the top level (except for SETQ, which on many systems does not work at the top level). Thus MINUS(5) will produce the answer −5; DIFFERENCE (12 7) will produce the answer 5; et cetera. So far we have not introduced any functions with *no* arguments, but if we had such a function, we would use parentheses after it, with nothing inside the parentheses. Thus if the function was called ALPHA, we would use it by writing the input line ALPHA( ). (This,

STANDARD FUNCTIONS

of course, is quite different from FORTRAN and ALGOL.) Here the symbols ( ) stand for a list containing nothing, or an *empty* list. Another way to produce an empty list is to write NIL; this is another of the uses of NIL. Thus **ALPHA NIL**, for example, would be the same as **ALPHA( )**.

1.9 Using subexpressions

The previous section still does not show us how to use a LISP system for anything more complex than a function of integer or real variables, such as **PLUS(3 5)** or **TIMES(6.5 4)**. In Chapter 2, we shall learn how to define our own functions and use them, but at this point we would like to be able to use expressions such as

(TIMES (DIFFERENCE 28 6) (PLUS 3 7))

and have the system print out 220. In the previous section we saw that we cannot simply write this expression as it stands, because TIMES is a function at the top level. On most LISP systems, however, there is another reason that we cannot write

TIMES ((DIFFERENCE 28 6) (PLUS 3 7))

as would have been indicated by the last section. This is that the convention, mentioned in Section 1.5, covering the evaluation of functions inside other functions, is *not* followed when a function, such as TIMES, is being used at the top level. Thus the above line would be equivalent to multiplying the list **(DIFFERENCE 28 6)** by the list **(PLUS 3 7)**, and *not* the number 28 − 6 by the number 3 + 7. This, of course, the TIMES function cannot do, and therefore it signals an error.

One way to avoid this problem is to use the function EVAL. If x is any S-expression involving integers, such as **(TIMES (DIFFERENCE 28 6) (PLUS 3 7))**, then we may construct the input line **EVAL(**x**)**, or on some LISP systems **EVAL (**x** NIL)** or **EVA1 (**x**)**, to find its value. Since x is now contained inside parentheses, it is not necessary (and would be wrong) to move the leftmost parenthesis to the right of the function name as discussed in the preceding section. We would simply write

EVAL((TIMES (DIFFERENCE 28 6) (PLUS 3 7)))

and the system would print out 220 (subject to the possible modifications mentioned above). Another construction, which will work on all LISP systems but for a more obscure reason, is (LAMBDA NIL *x*) NIL. Thus if we wrote

(LAMBDA NIL (TIMES (DIFFERENCE 28 6) (PLUS 3 7)))
NIL

the LISP system would likewise print out 220. Any arithmetic S-expression, of whatever complexity, may be tried out on a LISP system in this way.

It should, of course, be understood by now that extra parentheses cannot be inserted 'at will' in LISP as they can in FORTRAN and ALGOL. Thus the input line

EVAL((TIMES (10) (PLUS 4 8)))

would be incorrect, because, as noted in Section 1.5, the integer 10 would be considered as the name of a function (with no arguments).

Exercises

1 Rewrite the following algebraic expressions in the LISP notation:
   (a) $A * D + B * C$
*(b) $2 \sin^2 A - 1$
   (c) $-(A + B - C)$
*(d) $(B * C - A * D)/(C^2 + D^2)$
   (e) $p(A - B)$, where $p(X)$ is 0 if X is even and 1 if X is odd.
(Do not use P; use the REMAINDER function.)

2 What are the algebraic equivalents of the following expressions in the LISP notation?
*(a) (DIFFERENCE (TIMES B C D) (TIMES E F G))
   (b) (PLUS A B (TIMES C D) E (TIMES F G) (TIMES H I))
*(c) (MINUS (MINUS (MINUS Q)))
   (d) (QUOTIENT (PLUS (QUOTIENT A D) (QUOTIENT B C)) (DIFFERENCE (QUOTIENT A C) (QUOTIENT B D)))

3 Which of the following are S-expressions? State why the others are not S-expressions.
   (a) (PLUS (PLUS 4 5) 6)
*(b) (PLUS (PLUS 4 5 6)
   (c) (MINUS (MINUS (MINUS (TIMES A B C)))))
*(d) (QUOTIENT A,B)
   (e) (PLUS THE SQUARE ROOT OF A)
   (f) (TIMES A,B C,D E,F)

THE PROGRAMMER'S INTRODUCTION TO LISP

4   Consider the definition of an S-expression given in Section 1.2. Suppose that the counter mentioned in this definition has the value n when it encounters a certain left parenthesis. State a method, in terms of this counter, of determining which right parenthesis in the S-expression is the one that matches this left parenthesis.

5   *(a) Rewrite the algebraic statement $Y = A - (B - C * D)$ in the LISP notation.

(b) What is the algebraic equivalent of **(SETQ P (TIMES (PLUS Y Z) (DIFFERENCE Y Z)))** in the LISP notation?

6   The algebraic statement $X = Y = 0$, which sets both X and Y to zero, may be rendered in LISP by **(SETQ X (SETQ Y 0))**. This is because **(SETQ Y 0)**, considered as an *expression* (not a statement), has the value 0, and so this is what X is set equal to. In general, **(SETQ A B)**, considered as an expression, has the value B. (This topic will be taken up again in Section 3.4.) Using this convention, rewrite each of the following sequences of algebraic statements as a *single* S-expression:

(a) $J = I$
     $K = J + N$

*(b) $M2 = M1$
     $N2 = N1$
     $L = M2 + N2$

(c) $J1 = I1$
     $J2 = I1 + I2$
     $J3 = I1 + I2 + I3$

7   The following assignments in LISP are to be made one after the other. In each case, state whether the result has any meaning. (For example, if **(SETQ X (QUOTE Y))** is followed by **(SETQ Z (PLUS 6 X))**, then the second of these assignments is clearly meaningless, because it tries to add 6 to the symbol Y.)

(a) **(SETQ A (PLUS 3 7))**
*(b) **(SETQ A (PLUS A 7))**
(c) **(SET A (PLUS A 7))**
(d) **(SETQ B (QUOTE ALPHA))**

STANDARD FUNCTIONS

   *(e) (SET B (QUOTE BETA))
    (f) (SETQ C (PLUS 6 ALPHA))
   *(g) (SETQ C (PLUS 6 (QUOTE ALPHA)))
   *(h) (SETQ D (QUOTE 6))
    (i) (SETQ D (PLUS D D))
    (j) (SETQ D (PLUS (TIMES 8 7) (QUOTE 6)))

8 What value is given to ALPHA by each of the following?
   *(a) (SETQ ALPHA T)
    (b) (SETQ ALPHA (QUOTE T))
    (c) (SETQ ALPHA F)
   *(d) (SETQ ALPHA NIL)

9 What value is given to ALPHA by **(SETQ ALPHA (QUOTE (QUOTE 4)))**?

***10** Does the assignment **(SETQ ALPHA (PLUS 3 (LIST 4)))** have any meaning?

11 How many elements (atoms and sublists) are on the *main* list in each of the following cases?
    (a) (1 (3 5) 2 (8 7))
   *(b) (A (B C (D E) F (G H)))
    (c) (PLUS (TIMES 5 6) (TIMES (DIFFERENCE 5 3) 12) 2)
   *(d) (LIST 5 6 12 4)

12 What is the total number of sublists, sublists of sublists, etc., in each of the following lists?
   *(a) (6 (3 6 (7 (4 5) 8)) (9 3))
    (b) (((A 9)(B 7) C) (D 5))
   *(c) (QUOTE (S (3 5) (7 (9 8))))
    (d) (DIFFERENCE (QUOTIENT 27 3) (PLUS 1 (TIMES 7 (PLUS 3 (MINUS 2)))))

13 The following definitions are recursive. In each case, explain what is being defined by giving a non-recursive definition of the same thing.

(a) An A-expression consists of either a single integer, or else an integer followed by a comma followed by an A-expression.

*(b) The number n_k is defined by saying that n_k is twice n_{k-1}, where n_0 is defined to be 1.

(c) $D(P)$, where P is a person (living or dead), is defined to be a collection of people including P and all $D(Q)$ for each person Q who is a son or daughter of P (and no others).

*(d) $S(X)$, where X is a person, is defined to be a collection of people including X and all $S(Y)$ for each person Y such that X is Y's boss.

(e) $B(n)$, where n is an integer, is defined to be a collection of integers consisting of n and $B(n-1)$. (These integers may be positive, zero, or negative.)

14 A criticism of the definition of an S-expression given in section 1.7 is that the word 'sequence' is still undefined. Correct this by rewriting the definition, replacing the phrase 'a sequence of S-expressions separated by blanks or commas' by 'a Z-expression', where Z-expression is itself defined recursively. (Hint: see problem **13**(a).)

15 Suppose that we had a LISP function called CADD which added together two lists which represented complex numbers. Thus if (3 5) stands for $3 + 5i$ and (6 2) stands for $6 + 2i$, then **(CADD (QUOTE (3 5)) (QUOTE (6 2)))** would be (9 7), which stands for the sum of these complex numbers, namely $9 + 7i$. (A way of actually defining such a function and using it in LISP is discussed in Chapter 2.) Using this function, what value is assigned to ALPHA in each of the following cases?

*(a) (SETQ ALPHA (CADD (QUOTE (3 0)) (QUOTE (9 9))))

(b) (SETQ ALPHA (CADD (LIST 4 6) (DIVIDE 9 4)))

(c) (SETQ ALPHA (QUOTE (CADD (QUOTE (4 1)) ALPHA)))

STANDARD FUNCTIONS

16 What value, if any, is printed by the LISP system when presented with the following input?

(a) TIMES (8 2)

*(b) MINUS 5

(c) QUOTIENT (12) (4)

*(d) PLUS (18 0)

17 What value is printed by the LISP system when presented with the following input?

*(a) (LAMBDA NIL (PLUS (TIMES (MINUS 16) 2) 33)) NIL

(b) (LAMBDA NIL (LIST (QUOTE PLUS) 7 (DIFFERENCE 2 1))) NIL

*(c) (LAMBDA NIL (QUOTE (SETQ BETA (SIN BETA)))) NIL

(d) (LAMBDA NIL (DIVIDE (REMAINDER 29 10) (QUOTIENT 29 10))) NIL

18 What value is printed by the LISP system when presented with the input line (LAMBDA NIL (LIST (QUOTE SETQ) (QUOTE ALPHA) (LIST (QUOTE QUOTE) (DIVIDE (DIFFERENCE (TIMES (MINUS 5)(MINUS QUOTIENT 18 3))) (PLUS (REMAINDER 61 2) 0)) 10)))) NIL?

2 Constructing functions

2.1 LISP functions

The FORTRAN statement **FUNCTION INT(X, Y)** signals the start of a function definition, which has four essential parts:
 (1) The designator that a definition is to follow (the word FUNCTION, or PROCEDURE) in ALGOL or PL/1.
 (2) The name of the function (in this case, INT).
 (3) The specification of the parameters (x and y) in order.
 (4) The statements following, which actually define the function.

In LISP the designator that a definition is to follow is the word DEFINE. This is the name of a function. Thus we see another example of the general fact that in LISP there are 'nothing but functions'. The function DEFINE takes the place of FUNCTION in FORTRAN, for example, which is not a function name, but a keyword.

We must now give the rules for specifying the function or functions being defined. Before giving these rules, a word is in order about their arbitrariness. In several places in the LISP system there are functions which could have been constructed in any one of a number of different ways. Thus the function PLUS has an indefinite number of arguments, or parameters, and its value is their sum. We could, however, if we wanted to, define a function (let us call it ADD for the moment) which has *one* argument, which is a *list* of quantities to be added. Thus

        (ADD (QUOTE (1 2 3 4 5)))
and
        (PLUS 1 2 3 4 5)

would produce the same result, namely 15. When the PLUS function was first produced for the LISP system, a decision had to be made: should it have an indefinite number of arguments, or one argument

CONSTRUCTING FUNCTIONS

which is a list? We emphasize that there is no particular advantage to either of these two alternatives. The point is that the decision had to be made, and once made it was 'frozen' – all future LISP systems were constructed in the same way for compatibility purposes. But similar decisions were made for other functions in LISP; sometimes these decisions went one way, and sometimes the other. It is of no use to question why a function has its arguments arranged in a particular order; there does not seem to be any substantive advantage to any given order, but a rule must be made.

We now return to the DEFINE function. This function has *one* argument which is a *list* of functions to be defined. Each function to be defined is itself a list of two elements. The first of these elements is the function name and the second is the function description. Thus we might write at the top level (as an input line)

$$\text{DEFINE}(((\text{RHO } x_1) \ (\text{SIGMA } x_2) \ (\text{TAU } x_3)))$$

where x_1, x_2, and x_3 stand for three function descriptions. This would serve to define three functions named RHO, SIGMA, and TAU respectively. The expression $(((\text{RHO } x_1) \ (\text{SIGMA } x_2) \ (\text{TAU } x_3)))$ is the list of arguments of DEFINE. There is, in fact, only one such argument, namely $((\text{RHO } x_1) \ (\text{SIGMA } x_2) \ (\text{TAU } x_3))$, since DEFINE always has exactly one argument as mentioned above. This argument is itself a list of three S-expressions, namely (RHO x_1), (SIGMA x_2), and (TAU x_3). Note that RHO, for example, is taken to be the name RHO and not the quantity that RHO stands for.

Any legal specification of a function is permissible in DEFINE. In particular, we may define one function to be exactly the same as another. Thus the input line

$$\text{DEFINE}(((\text{RHO PLUS})(\text{SIGMA TIMES})(\text{TAU DIFFERENCE})))$$

would have the effect of defining RHO to be a function with exactly the same effect as PLUS, and similarly SIGMA as TIMES and TAU as DIFFERENCE. Thus

$$(\text{RHO}(\text{RHO}(\text{SIGMA } 2 \ 5)(\text{TAU } 4 \ 3)) \ 12)$$

would have the same effect (at inner levels) as

$$(\text{PLUS}(\text{PLUS}(\text{TIMES } 2 \ 5)(\text{DIFFERENCE } 4 \ 3)) \ 12)$$

THE PROGRAMMER'S INTRODUCTION TO LISP

– namely, it would produce the value 23. This is true because PLUS, TIMES, and DIFFERENCE are legal specifications of functions in LISP; they are, in fact, part of the standard collection of LISP functions.

2.2 Mathematical logic in LISP

The next question, of course, is how to specify the description of a function, such as x_1, x_2, and x_3 in the preceding example, in a more general way. This is where we make use of still another characterization of LISP, which, in addition to being a functional, symbolic, recursive, list processing language, is also a *logical* language.

Of the four essential parts of a function discussed in the previous section, part 1 is taken care of in LISP by the DEFINE function name itself, and part 2 consists of the first element of each function-defining pair. We shall now introduce a new 'function' with two arguments, which takes care of parts 3 and 4. In fact, the first argument corresponds to part 3 and the second to part 4.

The new 'function' is called LAMBDA. Thus

(LAMBDA (A B) (DIFFERENCE (TIMES A A) (TIMES B B)))

occurring in a function definition means: this is a function whose arguments are A and B, in that order; and the function is $A^2 - B^2$. In general, the first argument of LAMBDA is a list of the arguments of a function, and the second argument of LAMBDA is an S-expression which (presumably) uses these arguments.

The 'value' of a call to LAMBDA is itself a function description. It may, in particular, be used anywhere a function name may be used. If we give LISP the input line

(LAMBDA (A B) (DIFFERENCE (TIMES A A) (TIMES B B))) (6 3)

the LISP system outputs the number 27 (that is $6^2 - 3^2$). As usual, two S-expressions have been presented. The second of these is the list of arguments, (6 3), while the first, instead of being a function name, is a LAMBDA expression. In particular, LAMBDA can *not* have a value which is a number, a name, a list, etc.; and this is why

CONSTRUCTING FUNCTIONS

we have enclosed the word 'function' above in quotation marks. In the LISP terminology, LAMBDA is not, strictly speaking, a function, although it has arguments, and although the word LAMBDA appears first in its list, just as a function name would.

The LAMBDA construction has a long history in mathematical logic. It was invented by Alonzo Church, who wrote a book about it (*The Calculi of Lambda-Conversion*, Princeton University Press, 1941). In Church's notation, the use of LAMBDA above is $\lambda xy(x^2 - y^2)$; it must be carefully distinguished from $\lambda yx(x^2 - y^2)$. In LISP we must necessarily be a little more voluminous than this; for one thing, XY would be a separate atom, and not the pair of atoms X and Y.

We are now ready to define certain simple functions in LISP. Consider the input line (at the top level)

DEFINE(((P (LAMBDA (X) (TIMES X X)))))

This defines a single function, given by a list of two elements. The first of these elements is P, the function name. The second is (LAMBDA (X) (TIMES X X)), the function description. This description specifies that the given function has *one* argument, because there is only one atom, namely X, on the list which is the first argument of LAMBDA. This means that when we call P, it must have exactly one argument. After this input line we could, for example, write

P(7)

but not P(7 7) or P(3 5 2), because these would be calls to P with more than one argument. (At inner levels, our definition would be written (DEFINE ((QUOTE (P (LAMBDA (X) (TIMES X X)))))).)

The value of P(7) may be determined from the second argument of the LAMBDA expression. This expression specifies that, for the argument X, the value of the function is (TIMES X X), or X^2. It is very much like writing

INTEGER FUNCTION P(X)
P = X * X
RETURN
END

in FORTRAN, or **integer procedure** p(x); **integer** x; p: = x × x; in ALGOL. In fact there is a shorter construction in FORTRAN that does the same thing – the arithmetic statement function. In this case it would be

P(X) = X * X

written at the beginning of the program. In particular, the value of P(7) would be 49.

2.3 Parameters

In FORTRAN and ALGOL we have a notion of *formal parameters* and a different notion of *actual parameters*. If we write **FUNCTION P(X, Y, H)** in FORTRAN or **procedure** p(x, y, h); in ALGOL, then X, Y, and H are the formal parameters. If we then use the function in an expression such as $A - B * P(C - D, E/F, G)$, then $C - D$, E/F, and G are the actual parameters. The actual parameters may sometimes be expressions; the formal parameters may never be more complex than single identifiers, although these may stand for arrays or functions as well as variables. There is a correspondence between formal and actual parameters, and in the definition of the function given above, whatever the function specifies is to be done to X is done in actuality, if the function be used as above, to $C - D$. Similarly, Y corresponds to E/F, and H corresponds to G.

This notion of a one-to-one correspondence between formal parameters and actual parameters has a technical name in mathematical logic: *binding*. We would say that in this case X is *bound* to $C - D$, Y is bound to E/F, and H is bound to G. In LISP the same sort of thing goes on. Thus if we use the S-expression

((LAMBDA (X Y) (DIFFERENCE (TIMES X X)
(TIMES Y Y))) 4 3)

then X is bound to 4 and Y is bound to 3. The result is $f(4,3)$ where $f(x,y) = x^2 - y^2$; that is 16 − 9 or 7.

The above LAMBDA expression, as well as the ones given as examples in the preceding section, has the property that *every* variable which occurs in the second argument of LAMBDA is a bound variable (that is a parameter). This need not always be the case. For example, let us consider

(LAMBDA (A) (DIVIDE B A))

CONSTRUCTING FUNCTIONS

The value of this depends on the value of B. If B has been set to 15, then **(LAMBDA (A) (DIVIDE B A))** is a function $f(A)$ such that $f(15)$ is the list (1 0), $f(6)$ is the list (2 3), et cetera. (See the definition of DIVIDE in Section 1.5.) If B is something other than 15, then the corresponding function of A would be different.

In a LAMBDA expression such as this one, we say that the variable A occurring in **(DIVIDE B A)** is *bound* (because it appears as a parameter) and the variable B is *free*. Again we are studying a concept with a long history in mathematical logic. The distinction between free and bound variables becomes more complicated when a LAMBDA expression is used inside another LAMBDA expression. For example, in

(LAMBDA (A B) (TIMES A((LAMBDA (C) (PLUS C B)) A)))

the variable C in **(PLUS C B)** is bound, while the variable B in **(PLUS C B)** is free in the expression **(LAMBDA (C) (PLUS C B))**, but bound in the expression as a whole.

It is interesting to compute the actual effect of a LAMBDA expression such as the above. The subexpression **(LAMBDA (C) (PLUS C B))** is applied to the argument A. The result of this is **(PLUS A B)**. The entire expression, then, has the same effect as

(LAMBDA (A B) (TIMES A (PLUS A B)))

– that is, it is the function $f(a, b) = a(a + b)$.

Binding a formal parameter to an actual parameter and assigning a value to a variable are operations that, internally at least, have many similarities. In LISP, these two operations *are treated as* (almost) *identical*. In particular, whenever we assign a value to a variable with the SETQ or SET operations, we are in effect performing a binding. In the future we shall speak of a function call like

(SETQ Y 4)

as *binding* the variable Y to the value 4. Similarly

(SET (QUOTE X) (QUOTE (1 2 3)))

binds the variable X to the value (1 2 3).

THE PROGRAMMER'S INTRODUCTION TO LISP

2.4 List-processing functions

We are now able to use LISP in two ways: by making calls to system functions such as PLUS and TIMES, and by defining simple functions which are analogous to arithmetic statement functions in FORTRAN. In order to define more complex LISP functions, we shall have to have at our disposal a wider variety of system functions.

The functions CAR, CDR, and CONS* which we now introduce are often taught to students of LISP in the first or second lesson. This is because LISP is primarily a list processing language, and CAR, CDR, and CONS are the three primitive list-processing functions from which all other list-processing functions are derived.

The function CAR takes a list as its argument. Its value is the first element of the list. Thus

if X is (2 6 4 7)   then   (CAR X) is 2
if X is (2 (6 (4 (7))))   then   (CAR X) is 2
if X is ((2 6) (4 7))   then   (CAR X) is (2 6)
if X is ((((2) 6) 4) 7)   then   (CAR X) is (((2) 6) 4)

The function CDR takes a list as its argument. Its value is the remainder of the list with the first element removed. Thus

if X is (2 6 4 7)   then   (CDR X) is (6 4 7)
if X is (2 (6 (4 (7))))   then   (CDR X) is ((6 (4 (7))))
if X is ((2 6) (4 7))   then   (CDR X) is ((4 7))
if X is ((((2) 6) 4) 7)   then   (CDR X) is (7)

If X is an atom, then (CAR X) makes no sense, and in fact is undefined (and will cause an error). If X is a list containing exactly one element, then (CDR X) makes no sense from the definition as given above. However, we make the convention that in this case (CDR X) is the special atom NIL, which, as we recall, is also used to mean 'false'. This is another of the various uses of NIL.

The function CONS puts back together what CAR and CDR take apart. Its *value* is a list, and its *arguments* (there are two of them) are the result of CAR and CDR, respectively, applied to that list. Thus

* All LISP functions are pronounced as if they were English words. Thus CAR is 'car', never 'see-ay-ahr'. When there are no vowels, as in CDR, we do the best we can ('could-er' is an approximation).

28

CONSTRUCTING FUNCTIONS

if *X* is 2 and *Y* is (6 4 7)
then (CONS X Y) is (2 6 4 7)
if *X* is 2 and *Y* is ((6 (4 (7))))
then (CONS X Y) is (2 (6 (4 (7))))
if *X* is (2 6) and *Y* is ((4 7))
then (CONS X Y) is ((2 6)(4 7))
if *X* is (((2) 6) 4) and *Y* is (7)
then (CONS X Y) is ((((2) 6) 4) 7)

The result of CONS applied to any two arguments is as follows. The second argument should be a list; to get the value of CONS, append one more element on to the front of this list, namely the first argument of CONS (which may be anything, including an atom).

The above definitions of CAR, CDR, and CONS are not complete. We shall, however, postpone their complete definitions until Section 2.12, where we take up 'dot notation'. At this point we shall be able to see how fundamental CAR, CDR, and CONS really are. Dot notation is not, however, essential to writing functions and programs in LISP.

The *second* element of any list *L* is the first element of (CDR L), that is (CAR (CDR L)). This may also be written (CADR L). The third element of *L* is the second element of (CDR L), that is (CADR (CDR L)) or (CAR (CDR (CDR L))). This may also be written (CADDR L). In general, most LISP systems will allow the user to create a special function name by writing *C* followed by any number of *A*'s and *D*'s up to a reasonable maximum (say 5) followed by *R*. Each *A* in such an expression stands for CAR and each *D* stands for CDR, and the *A*'s and the *D*'s are taken in order from left to right. Thus

(CDADDR Y) would stand for (CDR (CAR (CDR (CDR Y))))

The function APPEND puts two lists together in the normal way. Thus

if *X* is (1 2 3) and *Y* is (4 5 6)
then (APPEND X Y) is (1 2 3 4 5 6)

This is sometimes called *concatenating* the lists (1 2 3) and (4 5 6). Note that in this case (CONS X Y) would be ((1 2 3) 4 5 6).

29

THE PROGRAMMER'S INTRODUCTION TO LISP

2.5 Predicate functions

An ordinary (declarative) sentence in English has a *subject* and a *predicate*. Thus in the sentence

CATS DO NOT LIKE TO BE THROWN IN THE WATER

the subject is CATS and the predicate is DO NOT LIKE TO BE THROWN IN THE WATER. If a sentence such as this one is to be used as part of an exercise in logic, the predicate is taken as being either true or false. For example, if we also assert that JOHN LIKES TO BE THROWN IN THE WATER, then LIKES TO BE THROWN IN THE WATER is true of JOHN and false when applied to CATS (and we conclude, of course, that John is not a cat). This seems to be the historical root of the use of the term *predicate* to apply to any function in logic, or in a programming language, whose value can be, and normally must be, either true or false.

Predicates are common in programming languages, but they are usually not called predicates. The operators .EQ. and .NE. in FORTRAN and the operators = and ≠ in ALGOL are predicates in the same sense that the operators + and * are functions of two variables. In particular, we could construct a function EQUAL(A, B) which would have, as its result, the logical value .TRUE. (or **true**) if A was actually equal to B and .FALSE. (or **false**) otherwise. The same is true of the other relational operators in FORTRAN and ALGOL, such as 'greater than', 'less than or equal', and so on.

In LISP, a predicate normally has the value T for true or NIL for false. This is in line with what we have said earlier about the use of NIL rather than F. Like every other construction in LISP, a predicate is a function.

The function ATOM has as its argument an atom or a list. If the argument is an atom, the value is T; otherwise, NIL. Thus

    if X is 5   then (ATOM X) is T
    if X is (the symbol) Y   then (ATOM X) is T
    if X is (1 2 3)   then (ATOM X) is NIL

The function NULL tests whether its argument is NIL. If so, the value of NULL is T; otherwise, NIL. Thus

CONSTRUCTING FUNCTIONS

>   if *X* is 5   then   (NULL X) is NIL
>   if *X* is (1 2 3)   then   (NULL X) is NIL
>   if *X* is NIL   then   (NULL X) is T

Note that if *X* is a list with one element, such as (7), then **(NULL X)** is NIL, but **(NULL (CDR X))** is T. This is because, as we discussed in the previous section, **(CDR X)** is defined, in this case, to be NIL.

The function EQUAL tests whether its two arguments are equal. If so, its value is T; otherwise, NIL. Thus

>   if *X* is (4 6 (8 3)) and *Y* is ((4 6) 8 3)
>   then   (EQUAL X Y) is NIL
>   if *X* is (PLUS 2 2) and *Y* is 4
>   then   (EQUAL X Y) is NIL
>   if *X* is (PLUS 2 2) and *Y* is (PLUS 2 2)
>   then   (EQUAL X Y) is T

Note that it is not enough for the *values* of the two arguments to be equal. Thus the value of **(PLUS 2 2)** is 4, but **(PLUS 2 2)** is not 'equal' to 4 in the sense implied by the EQUAL function.

The function EQ is like EQUAL in some ways; see Section 2.13.

The function ZEROP tests whether its argument is zero. The letter P in ZEROP stands for 'predicate'. If the argument of ZEROP is zero, the value is T; otherwise NIL.

The function GREATERP (where P again stands for 'predicate') has two arguments. It is true if the first argument is greater than the second, and false otherwise (that is, its value is NIL). Thus

>   if *X* is 7 and *Y* is 9   then   (GREATERP X Y) is NIL
>   if *X* is 9 and *Y* is 7   then   (GREATERP X Y) is T

The functions ATOM, NULL, EQUAL, ZEROP, and GREATERP are examples of predicates, but there are many more predicates in LISP. We shall now turn to how predicates are used.

2.6 Conditionals

A *conditional statement* in FORTRAN or ALGOL is an IF statement. In LISP, instead of a conditional statement, we have, as usual, a conditional *function*. The name of this function is COND. In some cases, although not in all, we can 'read off' a call to COND and

THE PROGRAMMER'S INTRODUCTION TO LISP

obtain an English sentence starting with 'if', just as we can in FORTRAN or ALGOL. Thus

IF (P.EQ.5) GO TO 7   or   **if** p = 5 **then go to** j

make sense as English sentences. Similarly

(COND ((ZEROP S) (SETQ J 12)))

reads as 'If *S* is zero, then set *J* to the value 12'.

The function COND has an *indefinite* number of arguments. Each of these arguments is a *pair*; that is, it is a list with two elements. The first element of the pair is a condition, and the second element is a quantity or an action. (Pairs of this sort are quite different from *dotted pairs*, to be treated in Section 2.12.)

Conditionals in *programs* will be discussed in Chapter 3. We restrict our present discussion to conditionals in *functions*. These are less like the FORTRAN IF statement than they are like the ALGOL conditional expression, a feature of ALGOL which may be unfamiliar. Thus

m := **if** c > 5 **then** 7 **else** 10

has the effect in ALGOL of setting *m* to 7 if *c* is greater than 5 and of setting *m* to 10 otherwise. It does this, however, by setting *m* to the value of the expression **if** c > 5 **then** 7 **else** 10, which always has a definite value that may be calculated – in the same way that $x - y * z$ may be calculated. In fact, if we define $gtr(x, y)$ to be 1 if *x* is greater than *y* and 0 otherwise, then **if** c > 5 **then** 7 **else** 10 has the same value as $10 - 3 * gtr(c,5)$. Conditional expressions such as this may be 'strung out' in ALGOL; additional **if**'s may be added as much as necessary. Thus

if a > 65 **then** 10 **else if** a > 21 **then** 30 **else if** a > 5 **then** 15 **else** 0

is a valid ALGOL conditional expression with a rather obvious meaning.

This type of expression is the prototype for the conditional in LISP. Indeed, we may write

(COND ((GREATERP A 65) 10)((GREATERP A 21) 30)
((GREATERP A 5) 15) (T 0))

CONSTRUCTING PROGRAMS

to obtain exactly the same effect as the ALGOL expression above. This call to COND has four arguments. They are ((GREATERP A 65) 10), ((GREATERP A 21) 30), ((GREATERP A 5) 15), and (T 0). Each of these arguments is a pair. The action which LISP takes for a COND is to look at each pair in turn, from first to last. If the condition given in any pair is satisfied, LISP stops there and takes the value of the second argument of that pair as its value. Otherwise, it goes on to the next pair.

The test which LISP makes to see whether a condition is satisfied is *not* whether its value is T. It is whether its value is *anything other than NIL*. If the value is NIL, the condition is *not* satisfied; if the value is *anything else*, the condition *is* satisfied. Thus we might write

(COND ((CDR L) 2) (T 1))

The value of this would be 2 if L is a list with *more than one* element. As we have seen before, if L is a list with exactly one element, (CDR L) is NIL. Otherwise, (CDR L) will be something other than NIL, and the condition will be satisfied.

The last pair in the COND expressions above starts with T (true). This is a condition which is *always* satisfied. LISP makes no distinction between the last pair and any other pair. Therefore, the T must be inserted in order that the COND expression have a meaningful value at all. If *none* of the conditions given in any of the pairs which are arguments to COND is satisfied, the LISP system will produce an error message.

2.7 Recursive functions

We are now in a position to be able to define a large class of functions in LISP. The construction of these functions involves the formulation of recursive definitions.

Let us start with the recursive definition of factorials:

$0! = 1$;
$n! = n \cdot (n-1)!$

We could, if we wanted to, translate this into a FORTRAN program (which would not work, because FORTRAN does not allow functions to call themselves):

33

```
      INTEGER FUNCTION FACT(N)
      IF (N.EQ.0) GO TO 1
      FACT = N * FACT(N − 1)
      RETURN
    1 FACT = 1
      RETURN
      END
```

Or we could construct an ALGOL program, which *would* work:

integer procedure fact(n); **integer** n;
fact := **if** n = 0 **then** 1 **else** n × fact(n − 1);

We have purposely constructed this ALGOL program to use a conditional expression in order to observe the similarity between it and COND in LISP. Indeed, the LISP expression which expresses the sentence 'if n is zero, then 1, otherwise n times the factorial of $n - 1$' would be

```
(COND ((ZEROP N) 1) (T (TIMES N (FACT
   (DIFFERENCE N 1)))))
```

if FACT stood for the factorial function itself.

Before defining the factorial function, we shall discuss one technical point. There are five right parentheses at the end of the expression above. It is extremely important that there be exactly five; if the programmer writes one too many or one too few, the entire program in which this statement is imbedded 'blows up'; it is not interpreted correctly by LISP. Most complex expressions in LISP will end with a large number of right parentheses in this way, and it is therefore important to have a mechanical procedure to check that the right number of parentheses is used. The reader should develop a procedure that he can use with confidence. One possibility is simply to count all the left and right parentheses in the entire expression; there should, of course, be the same number of each. Some LISP programmers look backward through the expression and close any parentheses that have been left 'open' – that is that do not have a corresponding right parenthesis. Such a programmer might think to himself 'close DIFFERENCE, close FACT, close TIMES, close T, close COND' as he types a right parenthesis for each closing.

We are now ready to define our FACT function. It is

**DEFINE(((FACT (LAMBDA (N) (COND
((ZEROP N) 1) (T (TIMES N (FACT (DIFFERENCE
N 1)))))))))**

Here we have used the word FACT as the name of the function and also in the LAMBDA expression which defines the function. This is the usual way in which recursive functions are defined. The LAMBDA(N) specifies that the new function FACT has one argument; the symbol N is used for this argument in the description of the function as the formal parameter.

The placement of the parentheses again deserves mention. DEFINE, at the top level, is always followed by three left parentheses. We separate out the first two, so that if more than one function is defined, we can think of each such function as being preceded by a left parenthesis. A large number of functions which we shall define start in just this way: a function name, followed by LAMBDA and a list of variables, followed by COND. This brings us up to parenthesis level 5. The five right parentheses at the end bring us back down to parenthesis level zero. These are often separated, as we have done; one only needs to close parentheses on the last pair within the COND, insert a space (which will be ignored) and then type exactly five right parentheses to close the definition properly. If another function definition is to follow within the same DEFINE, we type three right parentheses instead of five, and then we type the next function definition.

We also note that if our S-expressions get too long for one input line, we can continue them onto the next input line. LISP recognizes S-expressions as having balanced parentheses; there are no rules about one statement per line or one line per statement, and no special card columns or continuation characters, as in FORTRAN. This property of LISP is shared by ALGOL and PL/1; we say that LISP programs are in *free field format*.

2.8 Recursive list processing

We can also construct at this point a number of recursive functions which operate on lists.

THE PROGRAMMER'S INTRODUCTION TO LISP

The basic functions which operate on lists are CAR, CDR and CONS, which have been introduced in Section 2.4. When we are writing a recursive function which operates on a list, our recursion tends to be taken on the basis of the functions CAR and CDR. We shall illustrate this in the case of the function ADD which adds the numbers on a list, as mentioned in Section 2.1. Suppose we want to define ADD in such a way that, for example,

if L is **(1 2 3 4 5)** then **(ADD L)** is **15**

If we were not using recursion, we would think of a pointer moving down this list, picking up a new number each time, and adding it to a continuously accumulating sum. Such a function, however, can also be constructed, in terms of recursion, CAR, and CDR. We recall that

if L is **(1 2 3 4 5)** then **(CAR L)** is **1** and **(CDR L)** is **(2 3 4 5)**

From this we should be able to see that **(ADD L)** is the sum of **(CAR L)** and ADD applied to **(CDR L)**, that is,

(PLUS (CAR L) (ADD (CDR L)))

This definition is, however, not complete. There are several equivalent ways to see this.

One way is to note that defining **(ADD L)** as **(PLUS (CAR L) (ADD (CDR L)))** is a *truly* circular definition. A computer, given such a definition, would get in an endless loop. Another way to see that this definition is incomplete is to consider what happens to small lists. If we started with a list of only one element, then **(CAR L)** would be that element, and **(CDR L)**, as we have mentioned before, would be NIL. It is not clear that **(ADD L)** is defined when L is NIL.

There are two rather obvious ways out of the dilemma. One would be to make a special case of the situation where L is a list with exactly one element. This can be tested by seeing whether **(CDR L)** is NIL. In that case, the 'sum' of all the elements would be simply the single element, that is, **(CAR L)**, and we would have

(COND ((NULL (CDR L)) (CAR L))(T (PLUS (CAR L) (ADD (CDR L)))))

The other way is to define **(ADD L)** when L is NIL after all, and to define it then as zero. Thus if L consists of one element, the normal

36

definition will give **(CAR L)** plus zero, that is **(CAR L)**. We would then have

(COND ((NULL L) 0)(T (PLUS (CAR L)(ADD (CDR L)))))

The second method is usually taken because it is shorter (and also, for that matter, faster). The complete definition of the ADD function now reads

DEFINE(((ADD (LAMBDA (L) (COND ((NULL L) 0) (T (PLUS (CAR L)(ADD (CDR L)))))))))

As before, the **LAMBDA (L)** specifies the ADD function to have a single argument, which is the list L.

We may define in a similar way a function MULTIPLY whose value is the *product* of all the numbers on a list of numbers. This is

DEFINE(((MULTIPLY (LAMBDA (L) (COND ((NULL L) 1) (T (TIMES (CAR L)(MULTIPLY (CDR L)))))))))

The most important thing about this definition, aside from the substitution of TIMES for PLUS, is the fact that when L is NIL, the value of the function is not 0, but 1. In general, the easiest way to check what the value of a recursive function of a list should be when the list is NIL is to run through the recursive definition for the case in which the list has exactly one element. Thus in this case we would have **(CAR L)**, which is the single element, multiplied by MULTIPLY applied to NIL. Since the answer should be **(CAR L)**, we deduce that MULTIPLY applied to NIL should give 1. In this way we can always determine what the value of a recursive function should be when applied to NIL, even though, in practice, it is not intended very often to apply that function to NIL. Sometimes, of course, there are shortcuts. For example, mathematicians are quite comfortable with statements like 'the sum of no elements is 0' and 'the product of no elements is 1'.

2.9 Sublists and recursion

The function ADD defined above does not work properly when the list L has sublists. For example, if L is (1 2 (3 4) 5), then **(ADD L)**

THE PROGRAMMER'S INTRODUCTION TO LISP

does not give the value 15. In fact, the execution of ADD in this case might lead to an error, since LISP would attempt to add the list (3 4), using the PLUS function, to a number – an operation which makes no sense.

We may, however, define a new function recursively, such that it will in fact form the sum of all the elements on the given list and on its sublists. Let us call this function ADD2. Thus

    if *L* is (1 2 (3 4) 5)   then   (ADD2 L) is 15
    if *L* is ((1 2) 3 (4 5))   then   (ADD2 L) is 15
    if *L* is (((((1) 2) 3) 4) 5)   then   (ADD2 L) is 15

The last example above shows that ADD2 should be capable, not only of examining the sublists of *L*, but the sublists of the sublists of *L*, and so on as long as necessary. In order to do this, a function such as ADD2 must allow for two different 'dimensions' of recursion. One of these treats the list itself, and the other treats the sublists.

To write a recursive function which works on sublists, we consider the functions CAR and CDR and the predicate ATOM. We use ATOM to check whether the *first* element of a list is an atom or a sublist. If it is an atom, we handle it as before; if it is a sublist, we use recursion on it directly. If the *second* element, or any other element, of a list *L* is a sublist, we pick up that element later, when we are considering (CDR L).

The steps which we take in order to construct ADD2 are as follows. As before, we define (ADD2 L) to be zero if L is NIL. If L is not NIL, then we try to determine what has to be added to (ADD2 (CDR L)) to get (ADD2 L). The answer depends on whether (CAR L) is an atom or not. If (CAR L) is an atom, what has to be added is simply (CAR L); otherwise, it is (ADD2 (CAR L)). Thus our definition reads:

    DEFINE(((ADD2 (LAMBDA (L) (COND ((NULL L) 0)
    ((ATOM (CAR L)) (PLUS (CAR L) (ADD2 (CDR L))))
    (T (PLUS (ADD2 (CAR L)) (ADD2 (CDR L)))))))))

The last pair within the COND expression involves two recursive calls to ADD2. These are the two dimensions of recursion mentioned above.

CONSTRUCTING PROGRAMS

To illustrate this function further, let us consider the following two values of L:

    1 (3 ((8 4) 7 (5 6)))
    2 ((1 (2 3)) ((8 4) 7 (5 6)))

In both cases, (CDR L) is (((8 4) 7 (5 6))). Therefore, in both cases, (ADD2 (CDR L)) is 30. In the first case, (ADD2 L) is 33, and this is obtained by adding 3 to 30 – where 3 is (CAR L). In the second case, (ADD2 L) is 36, and this is obtained by adding 6 to 30, where we have obtained the 6 by adding together the 1, 2, and 3 in (1 (2 3)) – in other words, performing (ADD2 (CAR L)).

2.10 Recursive predicates

A predicate, like any other function in LISP, may be defined recursively. In such a case, T and NIL can be used as the second elements in the pairs making up the COND expression.

    The MEMBER function is part of the standard LISP library. It has two arguments, an atom X and a list L. If X is a member of L, then (MEMBER X L) is T; otherwise, NIL. Thus

    if X is 5 and L is (2 5 8 9)   then   (MEMBER X L) is T
    if X is 6 and L is (2 5 8 9)   then   (MEMBER X L) is NIL
    if X is 1 and L is (1 1 1)   then   (MEMBER X L) is T
    if X is 3 and L is (1 1 1)   then   (MEMBER X L) is NIL

We shall now define the predicate MEMBER as a recursive function.

    As usual, the approach will be to consider (CAR L) and (CDR L). Clearly (MEMBER X L) and (MEMBER X (CDR L)) have some relation. In fact, they are the same, unless X is equal to the *first* element of L, that is (CAR L). If this is true, (MEMBER X L) is always true. Otherwise, it is the same as (MEMBER X (CDR L)). So we might write

    (COND ((EQUAL X (CAR L)) T) (T (MEMBER X (CDR L))))

But this definition, like the one in Section 2.8, is not quite complete. As before, there are various equivalent ways to see this.

    One way is to consider that a predicate always has the value T or

NIL. The definition above has provided for the function to have the value T, that is when X is equal to (CAR L). But nowhere has this definition provided for the function to have the value NIL.

Another way to see that this definition is incomplete is, just as before, to consider what happens when L is small. Suppose that L consists of exactly one element. If this element is X, then the value of MEMBER will be T. If it is not X, we would like the value of MEMBER to be NIL; but what we get is the value of (MEMBER X NIL). It is clear, then, that (MEMBER X NIL) should be defined to be NIL. We may say, if we want to, that 'a list with no elements in it has no members'.

After adding a test for L to be NIL, that is (NULL L), we obtain for our definition of MEMBER the following:

```
DEFINE(( (MEMBER (LAMBDA (X L) (COND ((NULL
     L) NIL) ((EQUAL X (CAR L)) T) (T (MEMBER X
     (CDR L))) )))))
```

As a check, we may verify that this definition provides for the value of the function to be sometimes T and sometimes NIL.

It is interesting to observe the placement of parentheses when more than one function is defined in the same DEFINE expression. We define ADD, MULTIPLY, and MEMBER all at once, as follows:

```
DEFINE((
   (ADD (LAMBDA(L)(COND ((NULL L) 0)(T (PLUS
     (CAR L) (ADD (CDR L)))) )))
   (MULTIPLY (LAMBDA(L)(COND ((NULL L)1)
     (T (TIMES (CAR L) (MULTIPLY (CDR L)))) )))
   (MEMBER (LAMBDA (X L) (COND ((NULL L) NIL)
     ((EQUAL X (CAR L)) T)(T (MEMBER X
     (CDR L))) )))))
```

2.11 Logical operators

The functions PLUS and TIMES correspond in LISP to the arithmetic operators + and * in FORTRAN. Similarly, there are functions AND, OR, and NOT in LISP to correspond to .AND. and .OR. and .NOT. in FORTRAN, or to $\land$, $\lor$, and $\neg$ in ALGOL.

CONSTRUCTING PROGRAMS

The function NOT has one argument. It has value T if its argument is NIL and value NIL if its argument is T. It also has value NIL if its argument is anything else. This makes it exactly the same as the NULL function (see Section 2.5); but both names, NOT and NULL, are kept in the LISP system.

The functions AND and OR have an *indefinite* number of arguments, just like PLUS and TIMES. As usual, NIL is taken to mean 'false' and everything else is taken to mean 'true'. Thus the value of AND is always NIL unless the values of *all* its arguments are non-NIL, in which case the value of AND is T. Similarly, the value of OR is always T unless the values of *all* its arguments are NIL, in which case the value or OR is NIL. Thus

```
(OR T T)  is T          (AND T T) is T
(OR T NIL) is T         (AND T NIL) is NIL
(OR NIL T) is T         (AND NIL T) is NIL
(OR NIL NIL) is NIL     (AND NIL NIL) is NIL
```

and similarly

```
(OR T NIL NIL T NIL) is T       (AND T T T T T) is T
(OR NIL NIL NIL NIL) is NIL     (AND T T NIL T T T) is NIL
```

We illustrate further the use of OR by writing a recursive function MEMBER2, which bears the same relation to the function MEMBER of the previous chapter that ADD2 bears to ADD. That is, MEMBER2 will check to see whether its first argument is a member of the list which is its second argument, *or any of its sublists* (or any of their sublists, and so on). Thus if X is 6 and

```
L is (2 5 6 9)        then  (MEMBER2 X L) is T
L is (2 (5 6) 9)      then  (MEMBER2 X L) is T
L is ((2 5)((6) 9))   then  (MEMBER2 X L) is T
L is (2 (2 (2)))      then  (MEMBER2 X L) is NIL
```

As before, this is a recursive function which examines sublists, and therefore we expect there to be two dimensions of recursion.

We start to write MEMBER2 just as we did for MEMBER. First, (MEMBER2 X NIL) will always be NIL. Next, we must ask what relation (MEMBER2 X L) has to (MEMBER2 X (CDR L)). The answer is that they are the same unless X is equal to (CAR L), *or* unless (CAR L) is a list and X (which, we assume, must itself be an atom)

THE PROGRAMMER'S INTRODUCTION TO LISP

is a member of **(CAR L)**. This decision clearly depends on whether **(CAR L)** is an atom or a list. If **(CAR L)** is a list, **(MEMBER X L)** will be true if *either* **(MEMBER X (CAR L))** *or* **(MEMBER X (CDR L))** is true. This is where we may use the OR function.

The COND expression that we want to use reads

> (COND ((NULL L) NIL) ((ATOM (CAR L))(OR
> (EQUAL X (CAR L)) (MEMBER2 X (CDR L)))) (T (OR
> (MEMBER2 X (CAR L)) (MEMBER2 X (CDR L)))))

We have actually used OR in two places. The other place covers the case in which **(CAR L)** is an atom. We have also used **(MEMBER2 X (CDR L))** in two places. At the risk of a slight extra complication, we shall now show how this COND expression may be shortened. Note that whether **(CAR L)** is an atom or not, we want to perform an OR applied to something and **(MEMBER2 X (CDR L))**. We can therefore, in *every* case, apply an OR to a *conditional* expression and **(MEMBER2 X (CDR L))**. The result is

> (COND ((NULL L) NIL) (T (OR (COND ((ATOM (CAR
> L)) (EQUAL X (CAR L)))(T (MEMBER2 X (CAR L))))
> (MEMBER2 X (CDR L)))))

and our final definition is

> DEFINE(((MEMBER2 (LAMBDA(X L) (COND ((NULL
> L) NIL)(T (OR (COND ((ATOM (CAR L)) (EQUAL X
> (CAR L)))(T (MEMBER2 X (CAR L)))) (MEMBER2 X
> (CDR L)))))))))

The functions AND, OR, and NOT which we have defined may be thought of as predicates, since their values are always T or NIL, and in fact are often called predicates. However, they are different from other predicates in that their *arguments*, as well as their values, are quantities that are normally either T or NIL.

2.12 Dot notation

The list **(A . B)** in LISP is a list of two elements, in a sense; but it is quite different from the list **(A B)**. To understand the difference, we

CONSTRUCTING FUNCTIONS

must return to the consideration of lists in the memory of the computer, as discussed in Section 1.7.

A list in LISP consists of a sequence of pairs. The first member of each pair is a pointer to an atom or a pointer to a sublist. The second member of each pair is a pointer to the next pair. Dot notation allows us to look at the pairs separately. In **(A . B)**, we have a single pair. Its first member is a pointer to *A*, and its second member is a pointer to *B*. Such a pair is called a *dotted pair*.

The list **(A B)** would be formed in quite a different way. First of all, there would be two pairs involved. The first pair would be a pointer to A and a pointer to the second pair. The second pair would be a pointer to B and, according to the definition, a pointer to the 'next' pair. In this case, however, there is no next pair. In many list processing situations, a pointer such as this contains zero – to denote the end of a list. In LISP, however, this is not done. Instead, *the special pointer that denotes the end of a list is a pointer to NIL*. Thus the second pair, in dot notation, would be

(B . NIL)

and the entire list **(A B)**, expressed in dot notation, would be

(A . (B . NIL))

A list with sublists, such as **(A (B C))**, may also be translated into dot notation form; in this case it would be

(A . ((B . (C . NIL)) . NIL))

The first pair would be a pointer to *A* and a pointer to the second pair. The second pair would be a pointer to (*B C*) and a pointer to NIL. What do we mean by a pointer to (*B C*)? We mean a pointer to the *first pair* in the representation of (*B C*). This pair is, of course, a pointer to *B* and a pointer to the second pair.

The convention that a pointer to the first of a set of pairs representing a list may be taken as a pointer to the list itself is extremely important in LISP and leads to a proper explanation of the fundamental functions, CAR, CDR, and CONS. To see this, let us consider a more general list, such as

(A B C D E)

in which *A*, *B*, *C*, *D*, and *E* may themselves be either atoms or sublists. The first pair in the representation of this list is a pointer to *A*

43

and a pointer to the second pair. The remaining pairs, beginning with the second pair, are in *exactly* the same format as if the list

(B C D E)

had been represented instead of (A B C D E). A pointer to the second pair in the original list may therefore be considered as a pointer to (a representation of) the list (B C D E). Thus the *first* pair in the representation of (A B C D E) consists of a pointer to A and a pointer to (B C D E). This is a special case of a general recursive definition of the pair representation of a list:

A list L is represented in memory by a pair consisting of a pointer to (CAR L) *and a pointer to* (CDR L).

Of course, since the definition is recursive, we should not interpret the above to mean that *L* is represented by one and only one pair, since (CAR L) and (CDR L) will themselves be represented by pairs. This definition is the real reason why the CAR and CDR functions are fundamental in LISP. In dot notation, CAR and CDR have very simple definitions; in fact,

if *C* is (A . B)   then   (CAR C) is *A*   and   (CDR C) is *B*

Similarly,

if *C* is (A . B)   then   (CONS A B) is *C*

Dot notation may be used anywhere within a LISP function or program for the creation of temporary lists and for various other purposes. It uses less memory space than list notation, although it must always be remembered that only *two* quantities may be dotted at a time – the notation (A . B . C) makes no sense, although (A . (B . C)) does. Every list which may be represented as an S-expression without dots (in what is called *list notation* as contrasted with dot notation) may be translated into dot notation, since each list consists of a sequence of pairs, each of which may be represented as a dotted pair. Not every expression in dot notation, however, may be transferred to list notation.

In Section 1.7 it was mentioned that on the IBM 700 series of computers, on which LISP was first implemented, each 36-bit word has two special 15-bit fields called the address field and the decrement field. In a dotted pair, the first element of the pair is put in the address field, and the second element is put in the decrement field. The

CONSTRUCTING FUNCTIONS

function name CAR means 'place Contents of Address field in (index) Register', which is what the LISP interpreter does on such a computer when it encounters CAR. The function name CDR, similarly, means 'place Contents of Decrement field in Register'.

2.13 Recursive functions of two lists

The construction of a recursive function which has two lists as arguments proceeds along much the same lines as the construction of a recursive function of one list.

As an example, we construct a definition for the function APPEND, which is a LISP system function. We recall from Section 2.4 that

if L is (1 2 3) and M is (4 5 6) then (APPEND L M) is (1 2 3 4 5 6)

We note that in this case

(CAR L) is 1   (CDR L) is (2 3)
(CAR M) is 4   (CDR M) is (5 6)

and seek to find relations between (APPEND L M) and APPEND applied to CAR and CDR of L and M.

There seems to be no relation whatsoever between (APPEND L M) and (APPEND (CDR L) (CDR M)), which in this case would be (2 3 5 6). However, there is a relation between (APPEND L M) and (APPEND (CDR L) M), which is here (2 3 4 5 6). In fact, the second is the CDR of the first. To recover (APPEND L M) from (CDR (APPEND L M)), we use CONS, which in a certain sense is the reverse of CDR. To use CONS we have to know what to add to the beginning of (CDR (APPEND L M)) to get (APPEND L M) – and this, as we can see, is (CAR L), which is in this case 1. Thus

(CONS (CAR L) (APPEND (CDR L) M))

is an expression for (APPEND L M).

This expression is not a complete definition, because it is circular. Following the guidelines laid down in preceding sections, we ask what happens when the list L is NIL – because it is L that is being

45

THE PROGRAMMER'S INTRODUCTION TO LISP

broken up into CAR and CDR. The answer is that **(APPEND NIL M)** is just *M*. We may therefore make the following definition:

DEFINE((((APPEND (LAMBDA (L M) (COND ((NULL L) M) (T (CONS (CAR L) (APPEND (CDR L) M))))))))

Similarly, we may define EQUAL in terms of EQ, which is a simpler and faster function which, in most LISP systems, works on *atoms* only. Given two lists *L* and *M*, the equality of *L* and *M* is related to the equality of **(CDR L)** and **(CDR M)**, and the equality of **(CAR L)** and **(CAR M)**. In fact, *both* of these pairs must be equal for *L* and *M* to be equal. Thus we might write

(AND (EQUAL (CAR L) (CAR M)) (EQUAL (CDR L) (CDR M)))

as a recursive definition for **(EQUAL L M)**, except that this definition must be preceded by a special handling of the cases in which L and M are NIL or are atoms. If L is NIL, then **(EQUAL L M)** is true if and only if *M* is NIL, that is, if and only if **(NULL M)** is true. We may therefore write

((NULL L) (NULL M))

as one of the pairs in our COND expression. (This type of shortcut, that is using a predicate, such as NULL here, as the second half of a conditional pair, is quite common when a predicate function is being defined.) If *L* is not NIL, the next simplest case is that in which *L* is an atom. In this case, *M* must be an atom and *L* and *M* must be equal using the EQ function. Thus

((ATOM L) (AND (ATOM M) (EQ L M)))

is another pair in our COND expression. If *L* is not an atom, it is a list, and in this case, unless M is an atom, we can check the CAR and CDR separately. Our final definition is therefore

DEFINE((((EQUAL (LAMBDA (L M) (COND ((NULL L) (NULL M)) ((ATOM L) (AND (ATOM M) (EQ L M))) ((ATOM M) NIL) (T (AND (EQUAL (CAR L) (CAR M)) (EQUAL (CDR L)(CDR M)))))))))

CONSTRUCTING FUNCTIONS

2.14 Type functions

On most computers, there is nothing within a memory word that distinguishes an integer from a floating point number or a character string. This property of computers is carried over into FORTRAN; it is not possible to call a function which determines what kind of data is stored under a certain variable name. In LISP, however, we have atoms, which are not just single memory words; they have associated with them various information, and, in particular, a *type*, which may be numeric or symbolic. Thus for each variable it is possible, in LISP, to determine whether it has been set to a number or not. This is done with the predicate NUMBERP. Thus

    if X is 5   then   (NUMBERP X) is T
    if X is (the symbol) RHO   then   (NUMBERP X) is NIL
    if X is (1 2 7)   then   (NUMBERP X) is NIL

We have already discussed another kind of type function, namely ATOM, which determines whether its argument is an atom or a list. There are two more type functions in LISP that apply *only* to numbers. They determine whether a number is fixed point or floating point, and are called FIXP and FLOATP. Thus

    if X is 7   then (FIXP X) is T   and (FLOATP X) is NIL
    if X is 7·5   then (FIXP X) is NIL   and (FLOATP X) is T

The following function is slightly longer than those which we have constructed so far. It should be seen not only as an example of the use of NUMBERP, FIXP, and FLOATP (which are relatively obvious) but as an example of further complication in the construction of functions. The function is called COUNTFIXFLOAT. It returns a list of two integers. The first is the number of fixed point numbers on the list which is the argument of COUNTFIXFLOAT; the second is the number of floating point numbers on this list. Thus

    if X is (T LAMBDA 5.6 3 (8 ((9.1 4.122 J) B) 6 3.1 RHO))
    then (COUNTFIXFLOAT X) is (3 4)

since there are three fixed point numbers and four floating point numbers on the list X.

47

THE PROGRAMMER'S INTRODUCTION TO LISP

```
DEFINE(( (COUNTFIXFLOAT (LAMBDA (L) (COND
((NULL L) (QUOTE (0 0))) ((ATOM L) (COND ((NOT
(NUMBERP L)) (QUOTE (0 0))) ((FIXP L) (QUOTE
(1 0))) ((FLOATP L) (QUOTE (0 1))) (T (QUOTE
(0 0))))) (T (SUM2 (COUNTFIXFLOAT (CAR L))
(COUNTFIXFLOAT (CDR L)))) )))
(SUM2 (LAMBDA (L M) (CONS (PLUS (CAR L)
(CAR M)) (LIST (PLUS (CADR L) (CADR M)))) ))))
```

This function also illustrates the use of another device in LISP: the use of a 'subroutine', in this case the function SUM2, which is defined *after* it is 'used'. Those who are familiar with other programming languages may question the order in which the two functions COUNTFIXFLOAT and SUM2 are defined, but in fact this definition is quite analogous to the separate compilation of functions in FORTRAN. The function SUM2 adds together two lists of the form required by COUNTFIXFLOAT, element by element. Thus

if X is (4 3)   and Y is (7 2)   then **(SUM2 X Y)** is (11 5)
if X is (6 0)   and Y is (1 3)   then **(SUM2 X Y)** is (7 3)

Exercises

1 After each of the definitions below, the input line **BETA (2 3)** is given to the LISP system. What value is printed out in each case?
  (a) DEFINE(((BETA (LAMBDA (X Y) (TIMES X X Y)))))
  *(b) DEFINE(((BETA (LAMBDA (P Q) (DIFFERENCE Q P)))))
  (c) DEFINE(((BETA (LAMBDA (B A) (TIMES
      (PLUS A B) (DIFFERENCE A B))))))
  (d) DEFINE(((BETA (LAMBDA (U V) (QUOTE (F G))))))
  *(e) DEFINE(((BETA (LAMBDA (F G) (QUOTE (F G))))))

2 Write a DEFINE statement that:
  (a) Defines a function P such that $P(n)$, for any integer n, is a list of three elements, namely the square, cube, and fourth power of n.
  *(b) Defines a function which is just like DIVIDE, except that the remainder appears first in the list, followed by the quotient.
  (c) Defines a function A such that $A(n)$ is the list (THE ANSWER IS n). Thus the value of (A 12) is (THE ANSWER IS 12).
  *(d) Defines a function of seven arguments whose value is the sum of all seven arguments.

3 What is the value of each of the following LAMBDA expressions?
  (a) ((LAMBDA (Q R) (TIMES 10 R)) 800 3)
  *(b) ((LAMBDA (P) (LIST P (QUOTE P))) 4)
  (c) ((LAMBDA (X Y Z)((LAMBDA (A B) (TIMES (PLUS A X) (PLUS B Y) Z)) 1 1)) 3 4 2)

4   In Section 1.9 it was mentioned that **TIMES((DIFFERENCE 28 6) (PLUS 3 7))** would not be an acceptable input line to LISP, but later in that section it was implied that an acceptable substitute would be **(LAMBDA NIL (TIMES (DIFFERENCE 28 6) (PLUS 3 7))) NIL**. In the light of what you now know about the function LAMBDA, explain, in your own words, why this would work while the other would not.

*5   What will the LISP system do if we present it with the input line **DEFINE((UPSILON QUOTIENT))**?

6   Which variables in the following LAMBDA expressions are free, and which are bound?
  *(a) (LAMBDA (A B C) (TIMES (PLUS A C) (PLUS B D) (MINUS E)))
   (b) (LAMBDA (ALPHA GAMMA) (PLUS ALPHA BETA GAMMA DELTA))
   (c) (LAMBDA (T U V) (LIST T U (QUOTE V)))
   (d) (LAMBDA NIL (MINUS (TIMES X Y)))

7   What is the value of each of the following expressions?
  *(a) (CAR (QUOTE (X Y Z)))
   (b) (CDR (QUOTE (X Y Z)))
  *(c) (PLUS 7 (CAR (QUOTE (2 8))))
   (d) (CAR (LIST (QUOTE (4 6)) 3))
  *(e) (CDR (LIST (QUOTE (4 6)) 3))
   (f) ((LAMBDA(X Y) (CAR X)) (QUOTE (5 8)) 3)
  *(g) (CONS 3 (LIST 7 8 1))
   (h) (CONS (LIST 3) (LIST 7 8 1))
   (i) ((LAMBDA (X Y) (CONS Y X)) (LIST 6) (LIST 7))
  *(j) (CONS (QUOTE CDR) (LIST (QUOTE P)))

8   Which of the functions which start with C, end with R, and contain A's and D's, will:
   (a) Give (3 4) when applied to (1 2 (3 4))?
  *(b) Give (3 4) when applied to (1 2 3 4)?

CONSTRUCTING FUNCTIONS

   (c) Give (6 3) when applied to (((4 (6 3)) 8) 7)?
   (d) Give 12 when applied to (5 ((12) 23 34))?
   *(e) Give (12) when applied to (5 ((12) 23 34))?

9 What is the value of each of the following?
   *(a) (ATOM (CAR (QUOTE ((1 2) 3 4))))
   (b) (NULL (CDDR (QUOTE ((5 6) (7 8)))))
   (c) (EQUAL (CAR (QUOTE ((7)))) (CDR (QUOTE (5 7))))
   *(d) (ZEROP (CADDDR (QUOTE (3 2 1 0))))
   (e) (GREATERP (QUOTIENT 7 3)(QUOTIENT 14 6))

10 For each of the following conditions, define a function of one argument L, using DEFINE, which has the value T if the condition is satisfied and NIL otherwise.

   (a) The first element of L is 12.
   *(b) The first element of L is an atom (not a sublist).
   (c) L has at most four elements (atoms or sublists).
(Hint: Use the fact that applying CDR to a list enough times eventually produces NIL. Also, (CDR NIL) is NIL.
   *(d) The second element of L is greater than the fourth.
(Assume that L has such elements and that they are atoms and numeric.)

11 Write a conditional expression (a use of COND) which:
   *(a) Gives NIL if L is an atom and T otherwise.
   (b) Gives the maximum of the two elements of a list (without using any functions, such as MAX, that have not been defined yet). Assume that both elements are present and that they are atoms and numeric.
   (c) Gives, for a three-element list L, the first of these three elements that is an atom, or the list (NONE OF THESE ELEMENTS IS AN ATOM) if this is the case.

THE PROGRAMMER'S INTRODUCTION TO LISP

12 *(a) Define a function C57 of one argument which is a list that specifies a condition; the value of the function is a list giving a conditional which is 5 if the given condition is true and 7 otherwise. Thus if X is (GREATERP K L), then (C57 X) is (COND ((GREATERP K L) 5) (T 7)).

(b) Define a function of one argument L whose value is a list specifying a conditional which is 1 if X is NIL, 2 if X is an atom (not NIL), and 3 otherwise, where X is the (symbolic) value of L.

13 (a) Define a recursive function COPY such that (COPY X N) is a list of N copies of (the value of) X. (Thus (COPY 3 6) is the list (3 3 3 3 3 3).)
(Hint: Use CONS. What is the relation between (COPY X N) and (COPY X M) where M is one less than N?)

(b) Write a single usage of DEFINE which defines two different functions, one a definition of COPY exactly as above, and the other a definition of a function called EXPON, which uses COPY, such that (EXPON X N) is an S-expression which evaluates as X^N.
(Hint: The value of (EXPON 3 6), for example, should be the list (TIMES 3 3 3 3 3 3).)

14 *(a) Define a recursive function FIBON such that (FIBON N) is F_n, the nth Fibonacci number. (The Fibonacci numbers are defined by $F_1 = 1$, $F_2 = 1$, and $F_n = F_{n-1} + F_{n-2}$ for $n \geq 3$.)

(b) Define a recursive function EAPPROX such that (EAPPROX X) is the xth approximation to e, the base for the natural logarithms. That is, it is $1 + 1/1! + 1/2! + \ldots + 1/x!$. Assume that the QUOTIENT function gives a floating point result when applied to floating point arguments.
(Hint: Derive a relation between (EAPPROX N) and (EAPPROX M), where M is one less than N.)

15 (a) Define a recursive function COUNT such that (COUNT L) is the number of atoms on the list L; assume that L has no sublists. Thus if X is (2 8 8 7 −4), then (COUNT X) is 5.

CONSTRUCTING FUNCTIONS

(b) Define a recursive function COUNTG such that **(COUNTG L N)** is the number of numeric atoms greater in value than N on the list L; assume that L has no sublists and that all its atoms are numeric. Thus if X is **(2 8 8 7 −4)**, then **(COUNTG X 7)** is 2.

16 *(a) Define a recursive function CDRN such that **(CDRN N L)** is equivalent to **(CDDD . . . DR L)**, where there are N occurrences of D in the CDDD . . . DR function.

(Hint: What is the relation between **(CDRN N L)** and **(CDRN M (CDR L))**, where M is one less than N?)

(b) Write a single usage of DEFINE that defines COUNT (as above), CDRN (as above), and a new function LASTHALF which uses COUNT and CDRN; the value of LASTHALF should be a list of the last n atoms on a list of $2n$ atoms. Thus if X is **(2 4 6 8)**, then **(LASTHALF X)** should be **(6 8)**.

17 Rewrite the functions COUNT and COUNTG of problem **15** above, so that the condition that L has no sublists is removed in each case. Thus if X is **(2 8 ((8 7) −4))**, then **(COUNT X)** is 5 and **(COUNTG X 7)** is 2, just as above.

*18 Write a function DEPTH such that **(DEPTH L)** is the maximum sublist depth of the list L. Thus if L is **(1 4 (2 6 (3 7) 8))**, then **(DEPTH L)** is 3, because the sublist (3 7) is three levels (of parentheses) deep. You may use the function MAX (discussed in Section 4.1); here **(MAX I J)** is the greater of the two numbers I and J.

19 (a) Define a function NOSUBS, such that **(NOSUBS L)** is T if the list L has no sublists, and NIL otherwise.

(b) Write a single usage of DEFINE that defines NOSUBS (as above) and a new function ALLLEFT, which uses NOSUBS, such that **(ALLLEFT L)** is T if all of the left parentheses in the S-expression which represents the list L are at the extreme left of that S-expression, and NIL otherwise. Thus, if L is **(((3 4) 2 1) 8 9)**, then **(ALLLEFT L)** is T, but if L is **((3 4) 2 1 (8 9))**, then **(ALLLEFT L)** is NIL because the left parenthesis immediately preceding the 8 is not at the left of the S-expression.

(Hint: What is the relationship between (ALLLEFT L), (ALLLEFT (CAR L)), and (NOSUBS (CDR L))?)

20 *(a) Define a function MEMBERN, using MEMBER (as defined in Section 2.10), such that (MEMBERN V L) is true if and only if (MEMBER X L) is true for *each* atom X on the list V, which has no sublists.
(Hint: What is the relation between (MEMBERN V L) and (MEMBERN (CDR V) L)?)

    (b) Write a single usage of DEFINE that defines MEMBERN (as above) and a new function ALLVARSUSED, which uses MEMBERN, such that, if L is a properly formed LAMBDA-expression, then (ALLVARSUSED L) has the value T if all of the LAMBDA-variables are used in the given definition, and NIL otherwise. Thus if L is the list (LAMBDA (X Y) (TIMES X Y)), then (ALLVARSUSED L) is T, because both X and Y occur in (TIMES X Y), but if L is (LAMBDA (X Y Z) (TIMES X Y)), then (ALLVARSUSED L) is NIL because Z does not so occur.

21 (a) Write a function INRANGE such that (INRANGE V MAXIMUM MINIMUM) is T if V is between MAXIMUM and MINIMUM, inclusive, and NIL otherwise. Assume that V, MAXIMUM, and MINIMUM are all numeric atoms.

  *(b) Write a *non*recursive version of the function NOSUBS of problem **19** above, such that L is restricted to be a list of exactly three elements (which may be atoms or sublists).

  (c) Write a *non*recursive version of the function MEMBER (as defined in Section 2.10), such that L is restricted to be a list of exactly four elements (which may be atoms or sublists).

22 Rewrite the MEMBER function of Section 2.10 in such a way that its definition uses AND, OR, and NOT, but not COND.
(Hint: What expression involving AND, OR and NOT is equivalent to (COND (x NIL) (y T) (T z)), for any predicates x, y, and z?)

23 Translate the following dot notation into list notation:
  *(a) (A . (B . (C . NIL)))
  (b) ((A . NIL) . NIL)

*(c) (NIL . (A . NIL))
(d) (A . ((B . (C . NIL)) . ((D . (E . NIL)) . NIL)))
*(e) (A . (B . ((C . (D . ((E . NIL) . NIL))) . NIL)))
(f) ((A . (B . NIL)) . (C . ((D . NIL) . (E . NIL))))

24 Translate the following list notation into dot notation:
(a) (W (X))
*(b) ((W) X)
(c) (NIL NIL NIL)
*(d) (V (W) X (Y Z))
(e) ((V W) (X Y) Z)
*(f) (((V) W X) Y Z)

25 Define a recursive function DOMINATE which takes two lists as arguments, the two lists being of the same form (that is the placement of the parentheses in their S-expressions is the same) and such that **(DOMINATE L M)** is T if each atom in *L* is greater than the corresponding atom in *M*, and NIL otherwise. All atoms may be assumed numeric. Thus if *L* is (5 3 (10 (9) 4)) and *M* is (4 1 (8 (6) 5)), for example, then **(DOMINATE L M)** is NIL, because, although 5 > 4, 3 > 1, etc., at the beginning of *L* and *M*, we have 4 < 5 at the end of *L* and *M*.

****26** Define a recursive function EQUALL such that **(EQUALL L)** is T if *L* is a list whose elements (at the top level) are all equal to each other (using EQUAL), and NIL otherwise. Thus if *L* is ((12 5) (12 5) (12 5)), then **(EQUALL L)** is T, while if *L* is ((3 (6 9)) (3 (6 9)) (3 (6 9)) (3 (6 8))), then **(EQUALL L)** is NIL.

27 What is the value of each of the following?
*(a) (NUMBERP (PLUS 4 (TIMES 3 2)))
(b) (NUMBERP (CADR (QUOTE (MINUS 1))))
*(c) (NUMBERP (CAR (QUOTE (MINUS 1))))
(d) (NUMBERP (QUOTE (MINUS 1)))

(e) (NUMBERP (MINUS 1))
*(f) (NUMBERP −1)

28 Write a function GREATERFIXFLOAT such that **(GREATERFIXFLOAT X)** is T if the list *X* contains more fixed point than floating point numbers (at all levels) and NIL otherwise. The atoms on the list *X* are not necessarily assumed to be numeric.

3 Constructing programs

3.1 LISP programs

A LISP *program* is written in such a way that it may be substituted for the description of a function. This is done by the use of the special function PROG, which has an indefinite number of arguments.

A PROG expression is usually found as the second argument of a LAMBDA expression (note that we *cannot* substitute PROG for LAMBDA directly). It can, however, also be used elsewhere.

The arguments of the PROG embody the various constituents of a FORTRAN or ALGOL program. These are as follows:

(1) *Declarations.* The *first* argument of PROG is a list of variables which will be used in this PROG and which have to be defined at this point (not including, of course, the parameters). These are called the *program variables*. As in ALGOL, *every* symbol used in a LISP program must be defined; on the other hand, symbols are not declared as integer, floating point, etc., because the type of a symbol may change as the program is going on. Any symbol, of course, may represent a list, and lists may be used in place of arrays. (A very few LISP systems have an additional type, 'array', in addition to 'number', 'list', and so on.)

(2) *Statements.* These appear as arguments of PROG. We have already seen, in Section 1.3, what the assignment statement looks like; it is a SETQ expression or a SET expression. A subroutine call statement is simply an expression which uses the name of the subroutine as a function name, just as in ALGOL. Other types of statements are discussed below.

(3) *Labels.* These also appear as arguments of PROG. The arguments of PROG, therefore, are of three types: the first argument, which is a list of program variables; the statements, which are function calls; and the labels. A label is

always a single atom, and it is distinguished from a function call by this fact.

(4) *Transfer.* Instead of a GO TO statement, we have a GO function. It has one argument, which is a label. Thus

(GO SIGMA)

is a statement meaning to transfer control to the label SIGMA – that is to the statement immediately following this label.

(5) *Conditionals.* The function COND is used in place of an IF statement. There are two main differences between the use of COND in functions and in programs. In a program, the second element of each pair is not a *quantity*, but a *statement* (which may be any kind of statement). Also, the last pair does not have to start with T. If a COND expression in a program is not satisfied (that is if the first member of every pair in it evaluates to NIL), then the next statement in sequence is performed – just as in FORTRAN or ALGOL.

(6) *Returning a value.* This is done by the function RETURN. It has one argument, and that is the value to be returned. In FORTRAN and ALGOL this function is performed by using the name of the subroutine or procedure or function. If a function is called INT, for example, the FORTRAN statement INT = Z or the ALGOL statement INT:= Z; would impart to the INT function the value Z. In LISP, however, we would say simply

(RETURN Z)

Thus the name of the function is not involved. This type of return statement is similar to that found in the language PL/1.

As an example of all these notions, we consider the non-recursive program which might be written in FORTRAN IV or ALGOL to find the factorial of a positive integer:

INTEGER FUNCTION FACT(N)
I = N
J = 1

CONSTRUCTING PROGRAMS

```
1   IF (I.EQ.0) GO TO 2
    J = J * I
    I = I - 1
    GO TO 1
2   FACT = J
    RETURN
    END
```

integer procedure fact(n);
  value n; **integer** n;
  begin integer i,j;
  i:= n; j:= 1; k:
  if i = 0 **then**
  begin fact:= j; **go to** z **end**
  else begin j:= j × i;
  i:= i − 1; **go to** k **end**;
  z: **end**;

In LISP it would be

```
DEFINE(( (FACT (LAMBDA (N) (PROG (I J)
    (SETQ I N) (SETQ J 1)
K   (COND ((ZEROP I) (GO L)))
    (SETQ J (TIMES J I))
    (SETQ I (DIFFERENCE I 1))
    (GO K)
L   (RETURN J ) )))))
```

(handwritten annotation: declarations (not parameters))

Notice again the five right parentheses which are separated out at the end of the program. The first of these corresponds to the left parenthesis just before PROG. In general, after the last statement in a PROG has been written, three right parentheses are used if there are more function definitions to come within the same DEFINE expression, and five right parentheses otherwise.

3.2 List processing programs

It is also possible, in LISP, to write programs, using PROG, which operate on lists. In order to do this efficiently, however, we must use

THE PROGRAMMER'S INTRODUCTION TO LISP

techniques which are slightly different from those which we would use in ALGOL or FORTRAN.

To illustrate the difference, let us consider how we would process a list in an algebraic language. First of all, it is quite probable that the 'list' would not be a list at all, but rather a single array. In this case we would have an index which advances by 1 as we proceed through the array. To add all the elements in such a single array, we would write the following in FORTRAN or ALGOL:

```
      DIMENSION A(100)
      S = 0
      DO 1 I = 1, 100
    1 S = S + A(I)
```

array A[1:100];
s:= 0;
for i:= 1 **step** 1 **until** 100
do s:= s + A[i];

assuming that the array was called *A* and that it had 100 elements in it. Even if we had managed to construct a true list in FORTRAN or ALGOL, or (more likely) in assembly language, we would still have an index which advances through this list, except that now the index would be the location of the current item in the list. In either case, we may also refer to our index as a *pointer* to the current element of the list.

What do we have in the LISP language that corresponds to this use of a pointer? At first glance, nothing. Our elementary objects in LISP are atoms, which may be combined into lists, and the atoms may be numeric, but there is no correspondence between integers treated as atoms and addresses in memory. Thus, even if we are given an address *n*, we normally have no way of finding what atom or list is indicated by that address. We must therefore find some other way of processing lists in programs. What we do is to use the function CDR, which effectively removes the first element from a list after we have processed it.

To illustrate this use of CDR, let us rewrite the function ADD, of Section 2.8, as a program using PROG:

```
      DEFINE(((ADD (LAMBDA (L) (PROG (M N)
      (SETQ M L) (SETQ N 0)
```

CONSTRUCTING PROGRAMS

```
A (COND ((NULL M) (RETURN N)))
  (SETQ N (PLUS N (CAR M)))
  (SETQ M (CDR M)) (GO A) )))))
```

This function performs essentially the same task as the ALGOL and FORTRAN routines illustrated above do – it adds all the atoms on a list of numeric atoms. As an example of how ADD works, suppose that L is the list (4 3 6 2). Then the label A is passed five times during the course of the program; and the variables M and N have the following values at these times:

Iteration number	Value of M	Value of N
1	(4 3 6 2)	0
2	(3 6 2)	4
3	(6 2)	7
4	(2)	13
5	NIL	15

The value of N which is finally returned is thus $15 = 4 + 3 + 6 + 2$ – the sum of the atoms on the given list L.

The statement **(SETQ M (CDR M))** is to be especially noted. It is what effectively takes the place of advancing a pointer through the list M. Each time this statement is executed, an element is 'removed' from the beginning of this list. The LISP system does not actually remove this element; the list (4 3 6 2) stays in memory, but the value of the variable M is effectively a pointer to the middle of this list, that advances one position each time.

3.3 Constructing lists

When a program written in LISP produces a list as its value, or as an intermediate processing step, and this list is produced by a repeated process, one element at a time, it is important to produce the list in the proper direction. It is inefficient to build up a list by first computing its first element and then adding new elements on at the end. Rather, the *last* element of the list should be calculated first, and new elements added at the *beginning* of the list, so that the first element is added last. The reason for this is that LISP keeps track, at all times, of where the beginning of each list is, but not of where its end is.

61

THE PROGRAMMER'S INTRODUCTION TO LISP

Putting a new element on the end of a list involves going down the list, from first element to last, in order to find where the last element is, so that the new element can be added.

The function which we use to put elements on a list is CONS, rather than APPEND. It is true that APPEND will put a new element on either the beginning or the end of a list; thus

> if X is (7)   and Y is (8 3 6 2 5)
> then   (APPEND X Y) is (7 8 3 6 2 5)
> and   (APPEND Y X) is (8 3 6 2 5 7)

CONS, however, puts a new element on a list at the beginning, and does so much faster than APPEND. Thus

> if X is 7   and Y is (8 3 6 2 5)
> then   (CONS X Y) is (7 8 3 6 2 5)

We must remember, of course, that CONS cannot be simply substituted for APPEND. The first argument of APPEND is always a list, whereas the first argument of CONS is (usually) not a list.

As an example of a program which constructs a list, let us write a program called REVERSE which reverses a list. Thus

> if X is (1 2 3 4)   then   (REVERSE X) is (4 3 2 1)

The program REVERSE is defined as follows:

```
DEFINE(( (REVERSE (LAMBDA (L)(PROG (M P)
  (SETQ M L) (SETQ P NIL)
  A (COND ((NULL M) (RETURN P)))
  (SETQ P (CONS (CAR M) P))
  (SETQ M (CDR M)) (GO A) )))))
```

The coding of REVERSE points out a curious problem in LISP. Although the most efficient way to *create* a new list is in reverse order, from back to front, the most efficient way to *use* a list is in normal order, from front to back. This did not matter in the program REVERSE, and, in fact, was exactly what we wanted; but in most list processing situations in which an existing list is scanned in order to create a new list, we would like to process these lists in the same order. For example, we might like to construct a function which doubles every integer on a list of integers. If this function is called DOUBLE, then

> if X is (1 2 3 4)   then   (DOUBLE X) is (2 4 6 8)

CONSTRUCTING PROGRAMS

Partly in order to make this easy to do efficiently, many LISP systems contain a collection of functions which construct lists from other lists. These are known collectively as 'the MAP functions'.
The function MAPCAR is a typical MAP function. It has two arguments; the first argument denotes a list, and the second argument is the name of a function. MAPCAR applies this function successively to the elements of the list, and produces, as its value, a list of the results. Specifically, MAPCAR applies the given function to (CAR L), (CADR L), (CADDR L), (CADDDR L), and so forth, these being the elements of the list L. Thus we may, in particular, define (DOUBLE X) as above to be (MAPCAR X (QUOTE H)), where H is the function that doubles an integer. Specifically, if we have written

DEFINE(((H (LAMBDA (N) (PLUS N N)))))

then we may write

DEFINE((((DOUBLE (LAMBDA (X) (MAPCAR X (QUOTE H))))))

There are other MAP functions whose effect is slightly different. For example, there is MAPLIST, which also has two arguments, with the same significance, but which applies its given function to the list L itself first, then to (CDR L), (CDDR L), (CDDDR L), and so on.

3.4 The effect of a function

A two-dimensional array, or matrix, may be represented in LISP by a list of lists. For example, the N-by-N unit matrix δ_{ij}, where $\delta_{ij} = 1$ for $i = j$ and $\delta_{ij} = 0$ for $i \neq j$, $1 \leq i,j \leq N$, may be represented, for $N = 4$, by the S-expression

((1 0 0 0) (0 1 0 0) (0 0 1 0) (0 0 0 1))

Let us write a function UNITMATRIX to set up such a list, so that (UNITMATRIX N) is the N-by-N unit matrix:

DEFINE((((UNITMATRIX (LAMBDA (N) (PROG
(I J K L Z) (SETQ I N) (SETQ L NIL)
A (SETQ J N) (SETQ K NIL)
B (COND ((EQUAL I J)(SETQ Z 1)) (T (SETQ Z 0)))

63

```
(SETQ K (CONS Z K)) (SETQ J (DIFFERENCE J 1))
(COND ((GREATERP J 0) (GO B)))
(SETQ L (CONS K L)) (SETQ I (DIFFERENCE I 1))
(COND ((GREATERP I 0) (GO A)))
(RETURN L) )))))
```

This function uses two count variables, *I* and *J*, each of which is initialized to *N*. As the program proceeds, each count variable is decreased by one; if it is still non-zero, we return to the beginning of the loop. The list which is the result of the computation is constructed from back to front; its last element is formed first, then the next to last, and so on up to its first element. Note that the very first step is essentially **(CONS 1 NIL)**, the result of which is the list (1).

A good LISP programmer will be able to find ways to shorten this program. One way is by replacing the two statements

```
(SETQ J (DIFFERENCE J 1))
(COND ((GREATERP J 0) (GO B)))
```

with the single statement

```
(COND ((GREATERP (SETQ J (DIFFERENCE J 1)) 0)
   (GO B)))
```

This requires some explanation. The expression **(SETQ J (DIFFERENCE J 1))** is being used for two purposes. One is for its *effect*, which is to subtract 1 from the value of *J*. The other is for its *value*, which is the new value of *J*.

The use of functions for their effect as well as their value has both an advantage and a disadvantage. The advantage is that the description of a program may often be compressed, as above. The disadvantage is that in some programming languages the techniques which are used to make programs run faster do not work, in general, if routines may be used for their effect. In FORTRAN and ALGOL, for example, we have two different kinds of functions. One kind, called **SUBROUTINE** in FORTRAN or **procedure** in ALGOL, can be used *only* for its effect, and does not have a value. The other kind, called **FUNCTION** in FORTRAN or **real** (or **integer** or **Boolean**) **procedure** in ALGOL, has a value, and is supposed to be used only for its value. If it is used for its effect, this is

CONSTRUCTING PROGRAMS

deplored, and we refer darkly to 'side effects', as if a function were a dangerous drug.

In LISP, many of the standard functions may be used for both their value and their effect. This is particularly common in the case of the input-output functions, to be discussed in Section 3.11. A *defined* function, however (that is a function defined by the DEFINE function), *cannot* have one very important class of side effects: it cannot affect the values of the actual parameters supplied to it. In fact, in the ALGOL terminology, if a function is defined, using DEFINE, and then later used in a program, *it is called by value only*. Thus we cannot, for example, define a function INCREMENT by the statement

DEFINE(((INCREMENT (LAMBDA (X) (SETQ X (PLUS X 1))))))

and then expect to be able to use **(INCREMENT I)** later on in a program as a substitute for **(SETQ I (PLUS I 1))**.

3.5 Predicates written as programs

A predicate may be written as a program just as any other LISP function may be. It simply returns T or NIL, rather than some other value.

Programs which return T and NIL are especially likely to return T in one place and NIL in another. There is, of course, nothing which prevents us from having more than one RETURN statement in the same LISP program, just as we may have more than one RETURN statement in the same FORTRAN subroutine. (ALGOL is particularly clumsy in this regard; one may return from a procedure only by reaching its end, either normally or by going to a labelled **end** statement.) As an example of such a predicate, we shall now define a program which acts upon a list that represents a collection of playing cards.

The format of the list is as follows. Each card is represented by a list of two elements – first, the suit, and then the denomination, such as **(SPADE ACE)** or **(DIAMOND 10)** or **(CLUB 5)**. A 'hand' is then a list of such cards. The first function that we shall define searches such a list to determine whether it contains no spades (known as a

65

'spade void'). If there is a spade void, T is returned; otherwise, NIL. The definition is as follows:

>   DEFINE(((SPADEVOID (LAMBDA (L) (PROG (M P)
>   (SETQ M L)
>   A (COND ((NULL M) (RETURN T)))
>   (SETQ P (CAR M)) (SETQ M (CDR M))
>   (COND ((EQUAL (CAR P) (QUOTE SPADE))
>   (RETURN NIL))) (GO A))))))

This function returns NIL as soon as it finds a spade; if it finds no spades in the hand, it returns T. Thus

> if *X* is ((HEART ACE) (HEART KING) (HEART 3)
> (CLUB 4) (CLUB 3) (DIAMOND 6)) then
> (SPADEVOID X) is T
> if *X* is ((CLUB 10) (CLUB 9) (DIAMOND QUEEN)
> (HEART 6) (HEART 4) (SPADE QUEEN)) then
> (SPADEVOID X) is NIL

As another example of a conditional written as a program, we now define MOREHEARTS, whose value is T if there are more hearts than spades in the hand, and NIL otherwise. This program keeps two counts as it goes through the hand – one of the number of hearts, and the other of the number of spades. It compares the two only at the end; thus, in particular, there is only one RETURN statement. The definition is as follows:

>   DEFINE(((MOREHEARTS (LAMBDA (L) (PROG
>   (M P X Y) (SETQ M L) (SETQ X 0) (SETQ Y 0)
>   A (COND ((NULL M) (RETURN (GREATERP X Y))))
>   (SETQ P (CAR M)) (SETQ M (CDR M))
>   (COND ((EQUAL (CAR P) (QUOTE HEART))
>   (SETQ X (PLUS X 1))) ((EQUAL (CAR P)
>   (QUOTE SPADE)) (SETQ Y (PLUS Y 1))))
>   (GO A))))))

Notice, in particular, that there is no necessity for our RETURN statement to read precisely **(RETURN T)** or **(RETURN NIL)**. In this case, in particular, the value to be returned is precisely the value of

CONSTRUCTING PROGRAMS

(GREATERP X Y), since (MOREHEARTS L) will be true if this is true and false if this is false. Thus

> if X is ((HEART JACK) (HEART 9) (HEART 3) (SPADE 6) (SPADE 2) (DIAMOND KING))   then (MOREHEARTS X) is T
>
> if X is ((SPADE 8) (HEART ACE) (DIAMOND 5) (CLUB 10) (CLUB 9) (CLUB 5))   then   (MOREHEARTS X) is NIL
>
> if X is ((SPADE 9) (SPADE 4) (SPADE 3) (CLUB JACK) (CLUB 6) (CLUB 4))   then   (MOREHEARTS X) is NIL

The second COND statement in the above program points out another property of COND in programs. In a *function*, COND should have at least two arguments, because the last condition is generally T. In a *program*, there is no need for the last condition to be T, because if the last condition is not satisfied, we simply proceed to the next statement. In practice, most uses of COND in programs have only one condition in them. But, as the indicated COND statement shows, this is not necessary; even in a program, we may have more than one condition, although, as shown here, the last such condition does not have to be T.

3.6 Recursive programs

A recursive program in LISP means much the same as it does in any other language; it is either a program that calls itself, or one of a group of programs that call each other in a cyclic manner (that is program A_i calls A_{i+1}, $1 \leq i < n$, and A_n calls A_1).

Recursive programs are more common in LISP than they are in most other programming languages, because LISP programs so often act on lists. It is, of course, true that a LISP program which acts on lists will be 'less recursive' than a LISP *function* which does the same, because a LISP function will use recursion where the corresponding program uses looping without recursion. The treatment of sublists of a list by a program, however, is usually explicitly recursive; the corresponding non-recursive procedure would use a push-down list and would be much more cumbersome. As an ex-

67

THE PROGRAMMER'S INTRODUCTION TO LISP

ample of what is usually done, let us recode the function ADD2 of Section 2.9 as a program in LISP:

```
DEFINE(( (ADD2 (LAMBDA (L) (PROG (M N X)
  (SETQ M L) (SETQ N 0)
A (COND ((NULL M) (RETURN N)))
  (SETQ X (CAR M)) (SETQ M (CDR M))
  (COND ((ATOM X) (SETQ N (PLUS N X)))
    (T (SETQ N (PLUS N (ADD2 X)))))
  (GO A) )))))
```

This program calls itself only once, rather than twice as in Section 2.9. That is, there is here only one 'dimension' of recursion; this is typical of recursive programs in LISP.

The second COND statement in the above program points out still further possibilities for the use of COND in programs. Here we have a use of COND in a program in which the last condition is T. The effect is much the same as that of an **if** statement in ALGOL with the **else** clause, such as

if atom(x) **then** n := n + x **else** n := n + add2(x)

and is, like ALGOL, much less clumsy than if FORTRAN were used here, since in FORTRAN we would have to write something like

```
  IF (ATOM(X)) GO TO 6
  N = N + ADD2(X)
  GO TO 7
6 N = N + X
7 (next statement)
```

Also as in ALGOL, we may shorten the COND statement above by replacing it with

(SETQ N (PLUS N (COND ((ATOM X) X) (T (ADD2 X)))))

This time, the COND is of a type more frequently used in functions rather than programs. That is, it is used for its *value*, not for its effect. Even in a program, a COND used in this way follows the usual rules for COND in functions; in particular, if none of the conditions were satisfied, an error would arise, and thus the last condition is generally T.

68

3.7 Grouping functions

In FORTRAN IV we have statements such as IF (K.EQ.0) Y = X which allow us to perform one statement, in this case Y = X, if a given condition is satisfied. If we want to perform more than one statement, however, we must complicate our program slightly. If we wanted to perform both Y = X and Z = X, for example, when K was zero, we would have to do something like this:

```
    IF (K.NE.0) GO TO 7
    Y = X
    Z = X
  7 (next statement)
```

In ALGOL, however, we have a way of performing this directly. The statement we would use is **if** k = 0 **then begin** y: = x; z: = x **end**;. In this statement, the part between **begin** and **end** is called a *compound statement*.

The ALGOL statement here expresses the programmer's intentions more clearly than does the series of FORTRAN statements, and we would like to have this facility in LISP. Since statements in a program using PROG are executed one after the other, we would like to have a single statement which acts like a series of statements – two statements, in the above case. One way to do this is to collect the series of statements into a short 'program inside the program', using PROG. Thus we could write

```
(COND ((ZEROP K) (PROG NIL (SETQ Y X)
(SETQ Z X))))
```

where the NIL is necessary because the first argument of PROG must always be a list of variables, and here we do not need any (other than those which have already been defined).

Unfortunately, this is not a very efficient way of programming. Every time we use PROG, we take a certain amount of unavoidable extra time in the LISP system. In particular, even though there are no new variables, we must still look to see if there are any. In ALGOL, this problem is handled by defining two different kinds of groups of statements. One kind simply consists of a series of statements as above, and is called a compound statement. The other kind is called a *block*, and allows for declarations such as **real** q; or **integer** z;, although these must always occur at the beginning of the block. If a compound statement, rather than a block, is used in ALGOL, efficiency is improved. In LISP the use of PROG as above corresponds roughly to the use of a block in ALGOL. There is another function in LISP, called PROGN, which corresponds, even more roughly, to the use of a compound statement in ALGOL.

PROGN has an indefinite number of arguments. Each of these arguments is a statement in a program. The sole purpose of PROGN is to bring these together into a single statement, wherever a single statement is necessary – as in one of the pairs in a conditional. In particular, labels are not allowed (unlike the case of a compound statement in ALGOL). Thus

(COND ((ZEROP K) (PROGN (SETQ Y X) (SETQ Z X))))

would be an acceptable substitute for the COND expression above.

Like any function in LISP, PROGN has a value. Its value is the value of its *last* argument. Thus PROGN may also be used for its value as well as for its effect. This may be used in the construction of '*where*-expressions', which occur in certain algebraic languages (though not in FORTRAN or ALGOL). Thus

$$X = E + SQRT(E * E - C/A) \text{ WHERE } E = -B/(A+A)$$

is an efficient way of computing X according to the quadratic formula. In FORTRAN or ALGOL, we could write the statement computing E first, but this would obscure the fact that E is only a temporary result, and that X, not E, is what we are really trying to compute. In LISP, however, we could write

(SETQ X (PROGN (SETQ E (QUOTIENT (MINUS B) (PLUS A A))) (PLUS E (SQRT (DIFFERENCE (TIMES E E) (QUOTIENT C A))))))

The PROGN function is an extension of the PROG2 function, which is exactly the same as PROGN, except that it has only two arguments. The value of PROG2 is the last of these arguments, just as for PROGN. Some LISP systems have PROG2, but not PROGN;

CONSTRUCTING PROGRAMS

it is, of course, always possible to simulate PROGN with a use of PROG2 whose arguments are other uses of PROG2*.

As a further example of the use of PROGN, we write a program called OPPMAX which finds that element of a list M of atoms which is 'opposite' the maximum element of a list L of numeric atoms. Thus, if L is (3 7 13 9) and M is (T E S T), then (OPPMAX L M) is S, the third element on the list M, because this is opposite the third element on the list L, namely 13, which is the maximum element on that list. The definition is as follows:

```
DEFINE(( (OPPMAX (LAMBDA (L M) (PROG
(A B U V Y Z)
(SETQ A (CAR L)) (SETQ B (CAR M))
(SETQ U (CDR L)) (SETQ V (CDR M))
G (COND ((NULL U) (RETURN B)))
(SETQ Y (CAR U)) (SETQ Z (CAR V))
(SETQ U (CDR U)) (SETQ V (CDR V))
(COND ((GREATERP Y A)
(PROGN (SETQ A Y) (SETQ B Z))))(GO G) )))))
```

Here PROGN could, of course, have been replaced directly by PROG2.

3.8 The evaluation rule

The PROGN function is most succinctly described by saying that 'it does nothing but evaluate its arguments'. This phraseology is often used in LISP, although it does not mean quite what it says. To 'evaluate' a function would seem to mean that we are finding its value. In fact, when we evaluate (PLUS 2 4), the value is 6. But in LISP when we speak of 'evaluating' a function, we mean what in other programming languages would be called *executing* the function. The distinction here lies in the use of functions for their effect. If the expression (SETQ X Y) is to be 'evaluated', this does *not* mean simply that we calculate its value, which in this case would be the value of Y. The function, including all side effects, is executed whenever we evaluate it. In particular, evaluating (SETQ X Y) has the side effect of

* On some LISP systems, PROG2 is exactly like PROGN, except that its value is its *second* argument – even if it has more than two arguments.

setting *X* to have a new value, namely the value of *Y*. In the case of a function such as PLUS, however, evaluation is to be taken in the ordinary sense of calculating the value, in this case the sum.

It is often necessary to know exactly how the arguments of a function are evaluated. To illustrate this, let us consider

and
(SETQ Y (PLUS Z (SETQ Z 6)))

(SETQ Y (PLUS (SETQ Z 6) Z))

In each case we are using SETQ for its value, as well as its effect, in the inner expression. In the first case, we are adding the old value of *Z* to the value of (SETQ Z 6), which is 6. In the second case, we are adding the value of (SETQ Z 6) to the *new* value of *Z*. Thus the two answers will not necessarily be the same. The reason for this is that, in the second expression, the two arguments are (SETQ Z 6) and *Z*; and these are evaluated *in this order*. When (SETQ Z 6) is evaluated, *Z* gets a new value; when *Z* is evaluated, its value is this new value.

The *evaluation rule* is a recursive definition of what it means to evaluate a function. It is as follows:

To evaluate a function f (in the normal manner), *its arguments, both atoms and function uses, are evaluated in order, from left to right. The definition of f is then applied to this list of values, producing the value of f.*

The evaluation rule holds for all functions and programs that are defined by means of a DEFINE call, as well as for most of the standard functions, such as PLUS. The rule has, however, several exceptions. In particular, AND and OR are evaluated in a different way. The evaluation of (AND X Y) proceeds by evaluating *X* and then testing whether its value is NIL. If so, then the value of (AND X Y) must be NIL, and there is no need to evaluate *Y*. Only if the value of *X* is not NIL is *Y* evaluated. This not only saves time, it also prevents errors from occurring in many important cases. As an example, consider the definition of EQUAL in terms of EQ as given in Section 2.13. This definition contains the expression.

(AND (ATOM M) (EQ L M))

We recall that EQ works on atoms only. If *M* is *not* an atom, then (EQ L M) would give an error. When this use of AND is evaluated,

CONSTRUCTING PROGRAMS

we know that L must be an atom, but we know nothing about M. If the evaluation rule to be followed here were the standard one, (ATOM M) and (EQ L M) would always be evaluated, and our LISP system would give an error every time M is not an atom. Actually, however, (ATOM M) will be evaluated first. If it is NIL, then we are done; the value of (AND (ATOM M) (EQ L M)) will be NIL. Otherwise, (EQ L M) will be evaluated, but in this case M is an atom and we have no problem. Such usages of AND must be carefully constructed; in particular, it should be clear that AND is non-commutative here, that is that interchanging the arguments and writing

(AND (EQ L M) (ATOM M))

would be wrong, because it would not avoid the error case.

Incidentally, this special evaluation rule for AND is the reason why AND is not used instead of PROG2. If we tried to write (AND (SETQ Y X) (SETQ Z X)) instead of (PROG2 (SETQ Y X) (SETQ Z X)), it would work, most of the time – unless X happened to be NIL. In this case, the value of (SETQ Y X) would also be NIL, and we would never get the effect of (SETQ Z X).

The evaluation of (OR X Y) is the reverse of that of (AND X Y). That is, if the value of X is NIL, we proceed to evaluate Y; otherwise, the value of (OR X Y) is T, and Y is not evaluated. The treatment of AND and OR with more than two arguments proceeds by evaluating each of them in turn; the evaluation stops whenever an argument of AND is found to be NIL, or an argument of OR to be unequal to NIL.

3.9 The evaluation function

What if we have a variable whose value is a list, with an S-expression indicating that it may be treated as a usage of a function (that is the first element is a function name, and the other elements are the arguments) and we wish to find the value of this function as applied to the given arguments? In this case we use the function EVAL. Thus

if X is (PLUS 2 2)   then   (EVAL X) is 4
if X is (LIST 1 2 3)   then   (EVAL X) is (1 2 3)
if X is (QUOTE BETA)   then   (EVAL X) is BETA

THE PROGRAMMER'S INTRODUCTION TO LISP

Note that, just as before, (EVAL X)* where X is (PLUS 2 2) is not the same as (EVAL (PLUS 2 2)). This is a source of confusion, because (EVAL (PLUS 2 2)) actually has the value 4 – but not for the obvious reason. Just as (TIMES 7 (PLUS 2 2)) would be the same as (TIMES 7 4), so (EVAL (PLUS 2 2)) is the same as (EVAL 4) – but this is 4, because the value of any integer is itself. The value of (EVAL (LIST (QUOTE MINUS) 5)), though, would be −5, not (MINUS 5), because the value of (LIST (QUOTE MINUS) 5) is (MINUS 5) and the value of *that* is −5. To remove the confusion, we may write (EVAL (QUOTE (PLUS 2 2))) when we wish to refer to (EVAL X), where X is (PLUS 2 2).

The EVAL function corresponds to nothing in FORTRAN, ALGOL, BASIC or PL/1. It is one of the most important constituents of LISP that makes it more powerful than almost all algebraic languages. Using EVAL, we may execute 'statements' which have actually been constructed by our LISP program, and which may be different each time the program is executed. In most algebraic languages all our statements have to be laid out at the beginning into a program, and the form of these statements cannot change in the middle, while the program is running. A function like EVAL is, however, present in many other higher level languages, including SNOBOL 4, where it is known as CODE.

As an example of the use of EVAL, suppose that we wish to define a function whose name is the value of a variable which we call NAME. Suppose that we have also a variable called PARAMETERLIST whose value is the list of parameters for this function, and a variable called DESCRIPTION whose value is a list in function-call format which describes the function to be defined. (A list in this format, such as the list (PLUS 2 2) or (CAR (LIST (QUOTE ALPHA) 5)), is called, in LISP, a *form*.) Then we may define our function using EVAL as follows:

(EVAL (LIST (QUOTE DEFINE) (LIST (QUOTE QUOTE) (LIST (LIST NAME (LIST (QUOTE LAMBDA) PARAMETERLIST DESCRIPTION))))))

This constructs a list of the form (DEFINE (QUOTE ((n (LAMBDA p d))))), where n, p, and d are the values of NAME, PARAMETERLIST, and DESCRIPTION, respectively; then this list is evaluated,

* On some LISP systems, (EVAL X NIL) is used instead of (EVAL X).

CONSTRUCTING PROGRAMS

using EVAL. In particular, if NAME is (the symbol) DIFFERENCE, while PARAMETERLIST is (X Y) and DESCRIPTION is (PLUS X (MINUS Y)), then the evaluation of EVAL as above will serve to define the DIFFERENCE function in the normal way.

On many LISP systems there is another function, EVALQUOTE, which is like EVAL except that it takes *two* arguments, of which the first is the name of a function, and the second is a list of its arguments. Also, EVALQUOTE is an exception to the general evaluation rule of the previous section, in the following sense: the arguments of EVALQUOTE are *not* evaluated, but are taken exactly as they are (or 'quoted'). We say that EVALQUOTE *quotes its arguments*; SETQ, of course, is another example of a function which quotes only its first argument, rather than evaluating it.

We can now understand the reason for the special handling of parentheses at the top level in LISP as described in Section 1.8. The EVALQUOTE function is, indeed, constructed partly for the special needs of that part of the LISP system which reads functions and their arguments from cards or from a time-sharing terminal. The two S-expressions which are read at the same time by this part of the LISP system, called the *supervisor*, are exactly the two arguments of EVALQUOTE. Thus in such a system the supervisor is an extremely simple program (in most language processing systems, the supervisor is quite complex). All it has to do is to call EVALQUOTE, over and over, in each case reading its two arguments from the standard input device. This is called an 'EVALQUOTE supervisor,' and most LISP systems have it. Once more we have taken a well-known concept in programming, this time the supervisor, and expressed it as a function, as indeed almost all programming concepts are expressed in LISP.

3.10 Programs as data

Using the EVAL function, we may evaluate, not only single statements, but entire programs in LISP. A program, of course, is often a rather large list structure, and a single statement which constructs a program all at once using LIST and QUOTE would be a bit difficult to analyze. Instead of this, we may use variables whose values are list structures, and combine these variables so that the list structures they represent get progressively larger.

The function which we shall now define is called FOR, and serves a purpose analogous to that of the FOR statement in ALGOL (roughly, the same as the DO statement in FORTRAN). We shall define FOR in such a way that the value of

(FOR I J K L DESCRIPTION)

is a list of statements which could occur in a LISP program, and which corresponds to repeating the list of statements which is the value of DESCRIPTION, for *I* starting at the value *J* and increasing with a step size *K* until reaching a maximum value *L*. This will be analogous, then, to the ALGOL statement

for I:= J **step** K **until** L **do** description;

or to a DO loop in FORTRAN which starts with the statement DO *n* *I* = J, L, K for some statement number *n*, to be followed by DESCRIPTION as a group of statements with final statement number *n*.

We shall assume that DESCRIPTION is a list of the arguments of PROG, not including the first argument (the list of variables to be defined). The value of (FOR I J K L DESCRIPTION) will then also be a list of the arguments of PROG. As an example of how we want FOR to work, suppose that DESCRIPTION is ((SETQ D (CONS A D))); then the value of

(FOR A 1 B C DESCRIPTION)

would be a list structure such as

((SETQ A 1)
F (COND ((GREATERP A C) (GO G)))
(SETQ D (CONS A D))
(SETQ A (PLUS A B)) (GO F)
G)

If we analyze this piece of program we can see that it does, indeed, perform the statement mentioned in DESCRIPTION – that is, (SETQ D (CONS A D)) – several times, while varying *A* from 1 to *C* with a step size *B*, which, for simplicity, we shall assume to be positive. Also, we do not wish FOR to *evaluate* this program, using EVAL; this will presumably be done later.

There is one important difficulty in the construction of FOR. This is in choosing names for the labels *F* and *G*. How do we know that the symbols *F* and *G* themselves have not already been used as labels in the piece of program represented by DESCRIPTION? We don't. Also, we may call FOR several times, and then combine the given pieces of program into one large piece; we certainly don't want the labels to repeat themselves, because that would give us duplicately defined labels. The solution is to use a LISP function called GENSYM, which generates a symbol that is different from every other symbol generated this far. GENSYM has no arguments, and we may use it as many times as we like, always remembering that it will have a different value each time it is used.

We shall now define our function FOR, as follows:

```
DEFINE(( (FOR (LAMBDA (I J K L D) (PROG (W X Y Z)
   (SETQ X (APPEND D (LIST
      (LIST (QUOTE SETQ) I
      (LIST (QUOTE PLUS) I K)))))
   (SETQ Y (GENSYM)) (SETQ Z (GENSYM))
   (SETQ X (APPEND X (LIST
      (LIST (QUOTE GO) Y) Z)))
   (SETQ W (LIST (LIST (QUOTE SETQ) I J)
      Y (LIST (QUOTE COND) (LIST
      (LIST (QUOTE GREATERP) I L)
      (LIST (QUOTE GO) Z)))))
   (RETURN (APPEND W X)) )))))
```

When we arrive at the end of this program, *W* is the first part of the constructed program (up through **(GO G)** in the example, except that *G* has been replaced by a generated symbol) and *X* is the second part of the constructed program, starting with the value of DESCRIPTION. The APPEND function combines these into a single list; it is also used twice, earlier, to build up the list *X*. We could have defined the value of FOR as a single list, without using PROG at all; but the present version of the definition is more easily extended to incorporate efficiency in the resulting program. For example, we may modify FOR to test if the step size *K* is equal to 1, and, if so, to use a special function ADD1, available on some LISP systems, instead of PLUS.

3.11 Input-output

Statements in LISP which read and write data are just like any other statements in LISP: they are functions with arguments. It is not necessary, of course, to use any input-output functions at all in order to use LISP to solve a problem. As we have seen, all we have to do is to define a function, which corresponds to a main routine or a subroutine in other programming languages, and then 'call' this function, possibly with arguments; the LISP system will type or print out the result. If there are no arguments, we call the function with an opening and closing parenthesis; for example, if we have defined a function called Q with no arguments, we use Q( ) at the top level (or, what is the same, Q NIL, with a null list of arguments). But, in order to make LISP a more complete language, collections of input-output functions have been constructed.

There is less agreement over what functions to have in a LISP system for input-output than there is in connection with many of the other facilities of LISP. We shall now describe a particularly simple set of input-output functions, called READ, PRINT, and TERPRI, which are in use on many LISP systems.

The function READ has no arguments. Every time READ is called, the LISP system reads one entire S-expression. That is, it reads a (non-blank) character; if this character is not a left parenthesis, it is assumed to be the start of an atom, and the LISP system reads further characters until it gets to a blank, or other separation character, which is the end of the atom. If the first character is a left parenthesis, though, the system starts counting parenthesis levels and does not stop reading until it finishes an entire S-expression. (This, incidentally, is one disadvantage of LISP: an error in a single input card or input line can very easily prevent all other input from being read, particularly if the error involves leaving out a right parenthesis.) The value of READ is then the resulting S-expression.

As an example, if our input line were

2 5 (PLUS 3 6)

and we used the statements

(SETQ X (PLUS (READ) (READ))) (SETQ Y (READ))

then X would be set to 7 and Y would be set to the list **(PLUS 3 6)**. Note that Y would *not* be set to 9; the READ function reads S-expressions but does not evaluate them. As a slightly more complicated example, if our input line were

(PLUS (READ) (READ)) 2 6

and we used the statement **(EVAL (READ))**, its value would be 8. The expression **(PLUS (READ) (READ))** would be evaluated, or executed, and this execution would cause the next two S-expressions, namely 2 and 6, to be read and added. Incidentally, the EVALQUOTE supervisor, discussed in Section 3.9, may be defined by **(EVALQUOTE (READ) (READ))**.

The function PRINT has one argument, and it prints the S-expression of that argument. If we use PRINT at the top level, the S-expression is printed *twice*. The reason for this is that PRINT (and also READ, for that matter), besides being used for its effect, also has a value; and its value is the value of its argument. Thus if we set X equal to (1 2 3) and then write

PRINT(X)

at the top level, the first thing that happens is that X is printed, as directed by the PRINT function, that is (1 2 3) is printed; and then the LISP system does what it always does at the top level: it prints out the value of the called function, which is the value of X in this case, so that (1 2 3) is printed again. This difficulty, of course, disappears when PRINT is used normally, not at the top level; in fact, it is often used inside a program on a temporary basis, to print intermediate results while the program is being checked.

On a time-sharing system which allows the printing of individual characters, one at a time, PRINT is the only output function that is needed. Many time-sharing systems, however, as well as all systems that use a line printer for output, require an entire line to be printed at once. In this case, if we wish to use PRINT several times in the course of one line, then PRINT cannot actually cause printing, but only puts characters into a special character string in memory, which is then printed as soon as it reaches a certain length. Under these conditions, after we have finished the last use of PRINT in our entire program, this special character string will, in general, contain characters to be printed that have not been printed yet. The function TERPRI ('terminate printing') prints these characters. It is used at the end of a LISP program; it may also be used in the middle, just before a PRINT statement that we want to produce output at the beginning of a line.

Exercises

1 Consider the LISP program illustrated in Section 3.1.
   (a) What are the program variables?
   *(b) How many labels are there, and what are they?
   (c) Rewrite the last use of SETQ, using the function SET.
   *(d) One of the uses of the GO function in this program is unnecessary. Find it, and rewrite the program without it.

2 What function is computed by the following LISP program?
DEFINE(((X (LAMBDA (A B) (PROG (C D)
  (SETQ D B) (SETQ C 1)
  BACK (COND ((ZEROP D) (GO FORWARD)))
  (SETQ C (TIMES C A))
  (SETQ D (DIFFERENCE D 1))
  (GO BACK)
  FORWARD (RETURN C))))))

*3 Define a LISP program IND with parameters X and L which returns the smallest integer N such that X occurs as the Nth element of the list L, and zero if X does not occur in L. Thus

if X is 5 and L is (4 5 6 5 8)   then   (IND X L) is 2

if X is (5 (6 7)) and L is (2 (5 (6 4)) 3 (5 (6 7))) then (IND X L) is 4

if X is 9 and L is (1 2 3 4 5)   then   (IND X L) is 0

4 Suppose that we wish to go through a list with 'step size' greater than 1. As a specific example, let L be a list whose initial value is

THE PROGRAMMER'S INTRODUCTION TO LISP

(15 20 25 30 35 40 45 50 55 60). What statement may we insert in a loop in a LISP program which, when executed repeatedly, will cause L to have successive values which are such that the corresponding values of **(CAR L)** are 15, 30, 45, and 60 (that is with a 'step size' of 3)? Use a statement with as few parentheses as possible.

5 Consider the following definition of a function called RS:

```
DEFINE((( RS (LAMBDA (L) (PROG (A B C)
    (SETQ A L) (SETQ C NIL)
  Y (COND ((NULL A) (RETURN C)))
    (SETQ B (CAR A))
    (COND ((ATOM B) (SETQ C (APPEND C (LIST
       B)))))
    (SETQ A (CDR A))
    (GO Y) )))))
```

*(a) If L is (2 (3 4) 5 6 (7 8)), what is **(RS L)**?

(b) What does RS do, in general?

(c) Let us modify RS by changing **(APPEND C (LIST B))** to **(CONS B C)**, and by changing **(RETURN C)** to **(RETURN (REVERSE C))**, where REVERSE is as defined in section 3.3. Show why the new version of RS does the same thing as the original version.

*(d) Is the new version of RS faster or slower than the old version? Why?

6 Write a LISP program, using one of the MAP functions, which does the same thing as the function of the preceding problem.

*7 The statement $I = J = K = 0$ is permitted in some extended versions of FORTRAN as a substitute for the three statements $I = 0, J = 0,$ and $K = 0$ in succession. Using what we already know about LISP, is it possible for us to write a single statement which may be used similarly in a LISP program as a substitute for **(SETQ I 0)**, **(SETQ J 0)**, and **(SETQ K 0)** in succession? Explain.

8 What variables are set to what values by **(SET (SET X (QUOTE Y)) (QUOTE Z))**? Why?

CONSTRUCTING PROGRAMS

*9 Write a LISP program ANYVOID, which acts on a list like SPADEVOID (see Section 3.5), but returns T if there is a spade, heart, diamond, or club void, and NIL if the hand contains at least one card in each of the four suits.

10 Write a LISP program EXTRALONGSUIT, which acts on a list like SPADEVOID (see Section 3.5) and returns T if the hand contains at least seven cards of the same suit.

11 Write a LISP program which acts on a list and returns T if *all* the left parentheses precede *all* the right parentheses in the S-expression of that list, and NIL otherwise.

*12 Write a LISP program which acts on two lists and returns T if the S-expression of the first list has the same number of parentheses in it as the S-expression of the second list, and NIL otherwise.

13 Write a LISP program to sort a list of numeric atoms, with no sublists, using the interchange method. That is, each atom is compared with the next one, and if it is greater, the two are interchanged. This process continues until we have gone through the entire list once without any changes.

*14 Write a LISP program INDEXMAX which returns the index of the maximum numeric atom in a list of numeric atoms with no sublists. Thus, if X is (2 6 20 19 4 18), then (INDEXMAX X) is 3, since the maximum atom on this list, namely 20, is the third atom on the list.

15 What new value does X have after each of the following?
   *(a) (SETQ X (PLUS (SETQ X 2) 3))
    (b) (SET (CAR (QUOTE (Y X))) (SETQ X 2))
   *(c) (SET (CADR (QUOTE (Y X))) (PLUS (SETQ X 2) 5))
    (d) (SET (SET (QUOTE W) (QUOTE X)) (QUOTE Y))

16 Which of the following uses of AND and OR will *never* produce an error message? (Remember that (CAR X) produces an error message if X is an atom.)

THE PROGRAMMER'S INTRODUCTION TO LISP

    *(a) (AND (EQUAL (CAR X) (CAR Y)) (ATOM X) (ATOM Y))
    (b) (AND (ATOM X) (EQUAL (CAR X) (CAR Y)) (ATOM Y))
    (c) (AND (ATOM X) (ATOM Y) (EQUAL (CAR X) (CAR Y)))
    *(d) (OR (NULL (CDR X)) (EQUAL (QUOTE Y) (CAR X)))
    *(e) (OR (EQUAL (CDDR X) (LIST 7)) (ZEROP (CADR X)))
    (f) (OR (NUMBERP X) (GREATERP X 10))
    *(g) (AND (NUMBERP X) (GREATERP X 10))
    (h) (OR (NOT (NUMBERP (CAR X))) (ZEROP (CAR X)))

17 What is the value of each of the following?
    *(a) (EVAL (LIST (QUOTE MINUS) (PLUS 3 4)))
    (b) (EVAL (LIST (CAR (QUOTE (ATOM X))) 6))
    *(c) (EVAL (LIST (QUOTE EQUAL) (PLUS 2 2) (TIMES 2 2)))
    (d) (EVAL (EVAL (QUOTE (QUOTE (PLUS 2 2)))))

18 What is the value of each of the following?
    (a) (EVAL (CONS (QUOTE GREATERP) (CONS 5 (LIST ((LAMBDA (X Y) (DIFFERENCE Y X)) 3 7)))))
    *(b) (EVAL (APPEND (LIST (QUOTE TIMES) (EVAL (LIST (QUOTE DIFFERENCE) 7 5))) (DIVIDE 34 10)))
    *(c) (EVAL (LIST (LIST (QUOTE LAMBDA) (CDDR Q) (CDR Q)) 256 NIL)) (where Q is (FISH OR CUT BAIT))
    (d) (EVAL (LIST (CADDR (QUOTE (FOUR SCORE AND SEVEN YEARS AGO))) (CDR (QUOTE (((X))))) (ZEROP 0)))

*19 Write a function which takes two function names as arguments and produces as its value a program which defines the second of these to be exactly the same as the first. Thus, if the function is called *A*, the value of (A (QUOTE TIMES) (QUOTE RHO)) should be the list (DEFINE (QUOTE ((RHO TIMES)))).

20 Write a program which acts on a list which defines a function; the program should return the value T if this function calls itself (in the given definition) and NIL otherwise. For the purposes of this problem a function will be counted as calling itself if and only if its definition contains its own name in the function position, that is the first element of some sublist at an arbitrary depth. (We could, with a little trickery, construct definitions which violate this rule.)

*21 Write a LISP program which reads an English sentence such as THE QUICK BROWN FOX JUMPED OVER THE LAZY DOG (note that each word will be read as a separate atom) and prints out the number of words in the sentence. The sentence is permitted to have parentheses in it, but these parentheses may not be nested; for example, the sentence might be HE WAS HERE (ALTHOUGH SHE WAS NOT) AND HIS SISTER WAS ALSO HERE (ALTHOUGH HER HUSBAND WAS NOT). The period at the end of the sentence is to be represented, in the input, by the atom P.

22 Write a LISP program which reads an English sentence, as in the preceding problem, and prints out the entire sentence, enclosed in two pairs of parentheses. Thus, for example, if the input is THE QUICK BROWN FOX JUMPED OVER THE LAZY DOG P, the output should be ((THE QUICK BROWN FOX JUMPED OVER THE LAZY DOG P)).

4 Further topics

4.1 Further arithmetic functions

We have now covered all of the really essential features of LISP. There are many other features of LISP that are present on some, but not all, LISP systems; these are often quite important (such as the COMPILE function) but they are best learned by reading the manual for the particular LISP system to be used. It remains to cover a number of minor functions in LISP, and, at the same time, to give further examples of LISP programs.

The function RECIP gives the reciprocal of a number. Thus the value of **(RECIP 4)** is 0·25.

The functions FLOAT and ENTIER in LISP do the same thing that they do in ALGOL. FLOAT converts an integer to real (floating point) form and ENTIER does the reverse. Thus **(FLOAT 7)** is 7·0 and **(ENTIER 7.0)** is 7. ENTIER can also be used on floating point numbers that are not integral; its value, in this case, is the greatest integer less than the given floating point number. Thus **(ENTIER 7.2)** is 7, and so is **(ENTIER 7.75)**. (The word *entier* means 'integer' in French.)

There is an exponential function, EXPT, in LISP. **(EXPT A B)** gives *A* to the power *B* as its value.

All of the above functions, of course, will only be present in a LISP system which allows numbers to be either fixed or floating point. As we have mentioned before, in such a LISP system, the type (real, integer, or whatever) of every atom is kept at all times, and therefore declarations, such as the REAL and INTEGER statements in FORTRAN and ALGOL, are not necessary in LISP, and in fact would be a mistake, since a variable may sometimes represent a floating point number, and at other times a fixed point number, in the same program.

Two important functions which take an arbitrary number of

numeric arguments, just like PLUS and TIMES, are MAX and MIN. The value of MAX (or MIN) is the largest (or smallest) of these arguments. Thus

>(MAX 3 7 11 2) is 11   (MIN 3 7 11 2) is 2
>(MAX 851 518) is 851   (MIN 851 518) is 518

The function ADD1, constructed in such a way that (ADD1 X) is exactly the same as (PLUS X 1), is included in LISP systems mainly for the sake of efficiency. Adding 1 to a numeric atom is very common in programs, and is more efficient than adding an arbitrary quantity in the machine language of many computers. There is also a subtraction function SUB1, such that (SUB1 X) is exactly the same as (DIFFERENCE X 1). Finally, we may mention the even predicate, EVENP, whose value is T for even numbers and NIL for odd ones.

4.2 Function definitions in programs

Just as in ALGOL (though not FORTRAN), it is possible, in LISP, to write a function which defines another function and then uses it. This is done by using the DEFINE function at an inner level. That is, the description of the given function – the second argument of LAMBDA – may itself contain a usage of DEFINE.

Choosing a name for an internal function defined in this way may cause some difficulties. It is not enough simply to choose an arbitrary name, such as *G*, because this might be the name of a function already being used in this LISP program. (Using *F*, the standard letter for a function, would be even worse, because *F* means 'false' in LISP.) We can, if we want to, use the function GENSYM described in Section 3.10, and use its value as the name of our internal function. However, if the function which defines this internal function is used several times, this will cause functions with several different names to be defined. This may overload the LISP system, which will usually have a certain maximum number of LISP functions (with different names) that can be defined at one time. A better solution is to pass the name of the internal function as a parameter. Thus we may use the statement

>(X A B C (QUOTE P))

to use a function called *X*, with parameters (the values of) *A*, *B*, and *C*, which, in the course of its operation, will define an internal function, with the name *P*. (Some LISP systems would use **(FUNCTION P)** instead of **(QUOTE P)** in the above line; FUNCTION is a word which specifically indicates that its argument is to be the name of a function, but is otherwise the same as QUOTE.)

There is still another approach which is simpler, in many cases, than those discussed above. We recall that the LAMBDA function does not have to be used inside a DEFINE; it may be used by itself (see Section 2.2). Thus

((LAMBDA (X) (TIMES X X X X)) 2)

is, for example, the function x^4 applied to 2, giving 2^4, or 16. If our internal function is used (internally) only once, we do not need to define it at all, but can instead use it in this way. Even if it is used more than once, we can define a variable whose value is a LAMBDA expression and then use it by using EVAL. Thus, for example,

(SETQ X2 (QUOTE (LAMBDA (X) (TIMES X X X X))))

would set the value of X2 to be the list **(LAMBDA (X) (TIMES X X X X))**, and then

(EVAL(CONS X2 (QUOTE (2))))

would evaluate this function, with the argument 2 – noting the parentheses around the 2, because the second argument of the CONS function is always a list. Most of the time, of course, we would expect an internal definition of this form to be made in some other way, not using QUOTE, so that a decision may be made by the defining function as to how the internal function will be defined each time.

The use of LAMBDA expressions in this way causes another difficulty if the internal function is recursive. The trouble here is that a LAMBDA expression does not include a name for the function being defined. The reason that this causes trouble is that a recursive definition of a function called *H*, for example, defines *H* in terms of other usages of *H*. If we do not know what the function is to be called, we have no way of referring to it recursively in its definition. This problem has no solution in terms of the functions we have introduced thus far, and hence there is a specially constructed function called LABEL which takes care of it. The LABEL function has two

FURTHER TOPICS

arguments; the first is the name of a function, and the second is a description of that function, usually a LAMBDA expression, in which this function name may be used. Thus we may apply the function $x!$, or the factorial of x, to 5 as follows:

((LABEL FACTORIAL (LAMBDA (X) (COND
((ZEROP X) 1) (T (TIMES (FACTORIAL
(DIFFERENCE X 1)) X))))) 5)

The result, of course, is 5! or 120.

4.3 Compiling

A LISP system works differently from most ALGOL and FORTRAN systems in that it is basically an interpreter, rather than a compiler. In some LISP systems, however, there is a function, called COMPILE, which may be used to compile a LISP function.

The advantages of compiling, of course, are mainly concerned with speed. Every function in LISP takes a certain amount of time to execute; if the function is compiled, this amount of time is shortened considerably. Compiling a function converts it into a series of instruction words in machine language, just like compiling in FORTRAN or ALGOL. If a function is not compiled, the only description of it inside the computer is as a list structure. This list structure cannot be executed directly by the computer, and therefore there must be a program, called the interpreter, in memory at the same time that this list structure is, which examines the list structure and performs the function which it specifies. The reason that this is slow is that the list structure usually specifies either looping or recursion, and, in either of these cases, the same list structure must be examined over and over again several times. For example, when we calculate the factorial of 8 using the recursive definition of the factorial function, we must examine the entire list-structure definition of the factorial function eight separate times. If we were to compile the factorial function, however, we would examine this list structure only once, in order to determine what instruction words to compile. Once this has been done, the list structure is no longer necessary; the object code, or collection of instruction words produced, takes its place.

Compiling a LISP function is different from compiling a FORTRAN program in one very important way. In most FORTRAN systems, the output of the compiler is an object program which is either punched on cards or stored on tape or drum or disk for use at some later time. At this later time, there is no need for the FORTRAN compiler to be in memory. The object program is loaded by the loader and it can then run all by itself, except for a few subroutines – mainly for input-output purposes – which are supplied by the FORTRAN library. In LISP, however, the object program needs to call subroutines which are fundamental components of the LISP system. In most LISP systems which have compilers, in fact, the entire LISP system is kept in memory while the compiled object programs are running. This, of course, puts a stringent limit on the number and size of functions that can be compiled. It is, however, used to advantage in the compiling process itself, which is thereby made faster – just as it is in FORTRAN compilers which stay in memory during execution of their output, such as WATFOR and WATFIV.

There are certain LISP programs which should not be compiled. In particular, if a program or function is constructed during the course of a job, and then executed – presumably only once – it is unwise to compile this program or function unless it is particularly complex and will be expected to take a long time to execute. Since the LISP system is always in memory while compiled programs are being run, it is possible to combine compiled and interpreted programs in the same run in an arbitrary way. In particular, we may compile a function which constructs other functions as list structure and then either evaluates them, using EVAL, or else compiles them.

The exact rules for the use of the COMPILE function with any given LISP system should be determined by consulting the manual for that system. There is one common problem which crops up in compiling – namely, the fact that if a function defines a variable and sets its value to something, it cannot, in general, use this value the next time it is called. Thus, if, for example, we wrote a function called Q and then decided to modify it so that it would automatically count how many times it was used, we might introduce a new variable, called COUNT, defined by the function Q, and a new statement, (ADD1 COUNT), in the description of Q. If Q were compiled however, this would not work, in general, because if COUNT has a value (say 17) after the 17th time it is called, the LISP system does not guarantee that, when Q is called again, this variable will still have the value 17. This is a problem which was faced in ALGOL and solved by introducing a designator called **own**; a variable such as COUNT is declared, in ALGOL, by an **own** statement, to indicate that it is Q's own variable and that the space it uses is not to be shared by other programs. In LISP the analogous function is called SPECIAL. By calling SPECIAL with one argument which is a list of variable names, we may declare these variables to be special in this sense, so that their values will be retained from one usage of a function to the next. There is also another function called UNSPECIAL which declares that certain variables are no longer to be treated as special. As usual, there is no distinction between declarations, such as SPECIAL, and executable statements, as there would be in FORTRAN or ALGOL; all functions are executable, and therefore take a certain finite amount of execution time.

4.4 Machine-dependent features of LISP

Most versions of FORTRAN do not contain features which depend on the particular computer on which the FORTRAN program is run. There are certain exceptions, of course, such as the FORTRAN II 'Boolean statements' with the letter B in column 1. But, in general, a serious and relatively successful effort has been made to keep FORTRAN machine independent, so that programs which have been written using one computer may be run on another with little or no change. The same is true of ALGOL, provided that one sticks to ALGOL rather than the ALGOL-like languages such as NELIAC, AED, and JOVIAL; and with the one really annoying exception of the keywords – in some versions of ALGOL these are enclosed in quotes, in others not.

LISP, though, is quite different in this regard. There are no standards for the LISP language as there are for FORTRAN, and the constructor of any LISP system is free to put it together any way he likes. The result of this is that almost all LISP systems have quite a few features which are machine dependent. If a programmer uses these features, of course, he must remember that it will not be easy for him to transfer his program to a different computer.

There are, first of all, the Boolean, or logical, functions on atoms

THE PROGRAMMER'S INTRODUCTION TO LISP

regarded as (full) words in memory: the logical AND, the logical OR, and the exclusive OR. These are represented in LISP by the functions LOGAND, LOGOR, and LOGXOR. (These should be pronounced 'lodge-and', 'lodge-or', and 'lodge-X-or' – not 'log-and', et cetera, to avoid confusion with logarithms.) When applied to *positive* integers, the values of these functions are actually machine independent; thus, for example,

   (LOGAND 3 6) is 2   (LOGAND 6 9) is 0
   (LOGOR 3 6) is 7   (LOGOR 6 9) is 15
   (LOGXOR 3 6) is 5   (LOGXOR 6 9) is 15

as may be determined by considering the binary bit patterns involved, on a computer of any word length. When the numbers to be combined are negative, however, the results will depend on whether the computer involved uses one's complement or two's complement arithmetic, or even (such as with the original LISP system, on the IBM 700 series computers) signed magnitude arithmetic. Besides the logical functions, some LISP systems also have functions which perform a shift instruction. These have two arguments – the number to be shifted, and the shift count, or number of bit positions to shift.

 The most obvious machine-dependent feature of a LISP system, of course, is a provision for including an assembler. The communication between LISP programs and programs written in assembly language is quite different from the case of algebraic languages. A FORTRAN object program, for example, is in the same format as an assembly-language object program, and both can be loaded by the same loader and subsequently executed. A LISP system, however, normally uses all available memory space at all times, and hence there is no room for large programs, such as the loader, that are only going to be in memory part of the time. The result of this is that assembly language programs written for use with LISP programs are not assembled by the standard assembler for the given computer, but by a special assembler called LAP (for LISP Assembly Program). Such an assembler uses LISP input-output, which is S-expression oriented, and thus the assembly language will be quite different from standard assembly language. An instruction with the mnemonic LOAD, for example, applied to a variable Y, is represented by the S-expression (LOAD Y), where LOAD now looks like a standard LISP function with Y as its argument. This, in turn, has the result

FURTHER TOPICS

that programs which have already been written and checked out in assembly language must be rewritten in the special LISP assembly language if they are to be used by LISP programs. Such an assembly language facility, however, is useful in LISP for the same reason that it is useful in FORTRAN: every so often there are tasks which simply cannot be performed in any higher-level language within the available time and space requirements, and must therefore be done in assembly language.

Still another machine-dependent property of a LISP system is the way in which it uses the available word length. We have seen in Section 1.7 that data structures in LISP are built up from pairs of pointers. In some computers, however, a single word is not large enough to hold two pointers. If the word is 12, 16, or 18 bits long, it can hold *one* pointer, and the LISP system can then use pairs of words, rather than single words. If the word is 24 bits long, however, there are two possibilities: we may either try to squeeze a pointer into 12 bits (thus restricting the total pointer range to $2^{12} = 4096$ words) and have two pointers per word, or we can use pairs of words as before, with considerable wasted space. The most comfortable word sizes for a LISP system are 32 and 36 bits per word. At the other extreme, when the computer has 48, 60, or 64 bits per word, there is room for *three* pointers in a single word: and some LISP systems actually use this organization in their own special ways.

4.5 Garbage collection

We have, in general, been learning how to *use* a LISP system, not how to *construct* one. Every LISP programmer, however, should know at least the basic facts about the programming technique known as garbage collection, which is fundamental to the construction of LISP systems and has found wide use in other list processing and string processing situations.

All of the list structures which we have considered up to now are free from cycles. We may, for example, have a reference to an atom *A*, together with a pointer to a reference to another atom *B* – this would give us the S-expression (A B) – but there is no provision for the second reference to point back to the first. If there were, the resulting list would have no S-expression; or, rather, it would have the

93

infinite S-expression (A B A B . . . with no right parenthesis. Such a list would be called a *circular list*. It is not possible to construct a circular list with any of the functions which we have introduced thus far, but most LISP systems have functions, called the 'replace' functions, which allow us to set up a circular list.

If a LISP system *never* made use of replace functions, but worked only with lists which have S-expressions, garbage collection would not be absolutely necessary. Under these conditions, the job of finding memory space in the computer for new lists would be comparatively simple. A large area of memory, called *free storage*, is set aside by all LISP systems to contain pairs of pointers. Each word (or, on small computers, each pair of words) in free storage would then, at all times, be on some list. If it is not on a list that is currently in use, then it is on a *list of available space*, which, at all times, contains exactly those words which are on no other list.

One of the disadvantages of LISP, however, is that it uses more time and memory space than it seemingly ought to, and, to mitigate this, all LISP systems actually make use of many kinds of lists, including circular lists, that do not have S-expressions. The replace functions allow this to be done in an arbitrary way, since they act directly on pairs of pointers. Each replace function has two arguments, X and Y, and sets either the address field or decrement field pointer (see Section 2.12) of X to the new value Y. The names of the replace functions are RPLACA and RPLACD respectively. Thus any pointer, anywhere within free storage, may be set to any value whatsoever, and, in particular, circular lists may be formed. Replace functions can also improve the efficiency of processing of S-expression-type lists; for example, they are used to construct a function called NCONC, which is a faster version of APPEND.

To see why this interferes with the continuous maintenance of a list of available space, let us consider the fundamental operations on such a list. When a new pair of pointers is needed for some purpose, it is removed from the list of available space and placed on some other list. When an *old* pair of pointers, which is no longer needed, is removed from a list, it would then have to be put back on this list of available space. Similarly, when an entire list is deleted, all the pairs of pointers it uses would have to be returned to the list of available space. The difficulty here is that if pointers can be set to arbitrary values we have no way of knowing, at any time, how many pointers

FURTHER TOPICS

point to a given pair, and thus we have no way of knowing whether that pair is really available. Thus, even if it is on a list that is being deleted, we cannot put it back on the list of available space, because, for all we know, it might be on some other list as well.

This, of course, creates an intolerable situation. We may still have a list of available space, but it will continue to get smaller and smaller as the program proceeds. Eventually, the list of available space will be exhausted, but there will still be words all over free storage which are available – and, seemingly, we have no way of knowing where these words are. Garbage collection solves the problem by actually finding out where the available words are and collecting them into a new list of available space. Thus the program proceeds 'like a jerky automobile' – every so often, everything stops while the garbage collection routine proceeds to collect the currently available words in free storage (the 'garbage') into a single list. Once that is done, the program can proceed again.

To find out where the available words are, the garbage collection routine first finds out where the *un*available words are. Every word that is not unavailable is then counted as being available. The unavailable words, of course, are the words which are already on some list, and the garbage collection routine therefore must scan all lists currently in use and determine which words they use. For this purpose a single bit per word is used; one value (either zero or one) means 'available', and the other value means 'unavailable'.

4.6 Miscellaneous topics

In addition to garbage collection, there are certain other topics with which every LISP programmer should have at least a passing acquaintance:

1 *EXPR and SUBR.* Every function in LISP is either an EXPR (pronounced 'ex-per'), a SUBR ('subber'), an FEXPR ('F-ex-per') or an FSUBR ('F-subber'). EXPR and SUBR stand for 'expression' (that is, S-expression) and 'subroutine', respectively, and refer to whether the function has simply been defined as a list structure in LISP or actually coded in assembly language within the LISP system as a subroutine of that system (or in machine language by the LISP

95

compiler). In the latter case, of course, it will be much faster; in the former case, it will take up less space in memory. EXPRs and SUBRs bind their variables in the standard way, whereas FEXPRs and FSUBRs can bind them in non-standard ways and thus can quote some of their arguments, have a variable number of arguments, etc., which EXPRs and SUBRs cannot.

2 *Property lists.* We have mentioned the fact that the type (fixed point, floating point, symbolic, etc.) of an atom is kept in memory at all times. The concept of type may be thought of as a special case of a *property*. An atom may have an unlimited number of properties; thus an atom called JOHN may have TYPE SYMBOLIC, SEX MALE, AGE 45, and so on. On many LISP systems, the properties of an atom are kept on a list known as the *property list* of that atom (except for TYPE, which is so important that it is almost always handled in a special-purpose manner for the sake of efficiency). The property list is a list of pairs, and these are very often dotted pairs; there are then general-purpose functions to search, insert, change, and delete property pairs. An advantage of this general approach is that the *name* of an atom is now also a property of it, and does not have to be handled separately. Thus the above atom might have NAME JOHN as well as TYPE SYMBOLIC, etc. More often, PNAME JOHN is used, the property PNAME (or 'print name') being used to emphasize the fact that the atoms in a LISP program are abstract objects, independent of their names, which need not be referenced unless and until they are printed or otherwise output. The *value* of an atom might also be a property under certain special conditions; thus an atom might have NAME (or PNAME) PI, and VALUE (or, usually, APVAL) 3·14159265. Such a value for an atom is independent of the binding mechanism. The definition of a function, also, is a property of that function.

3 *Arrays.* A very frequent criticism of LISP is one that is more properly made of all list processing: finding the kth element of a list, when k is known, is a very time-consuming process. The alternative – keeping at least some of our lists sequentially allocated, that is as simple (single) arrays are kept in FORTRAN – is very inviting, but, unfortunately, poses storage allocation problems that are extremely difficult to solve and that, in particular, are not completely taken care of by garbage collection. Nevertheless, some LISP systems

do have an array feature. It is recommended that this feature be used, if it is available, *only* by those who understand how the LISP system actually does its job, so that the aforementioned problems may be avoided.

4 *Character string manipulation.* Again, some LISP systems will have *very* rudimentary features for concatenating strings and for taking a constructed string name and using it as the name of an atom. This is done much better, of course, in SNOBOL, using the 'indirect reference' feature. The interrelationship between list processing languages, like LISP, and string processing languages, like SNOBOL, is mutual: string processing packages have been written in LISP, and simple systems that process S-expressions in somewhat the same way that LISP does have been written in SNOBOL. One interesting feature of the facility that some LISP systems have in this connection is that, just as in SNOBOL, one may use an atom whose print name is *any* string of characters – not just letters and numbers. This is called the use of non-standard print names.

5 *Macros.* The idea of using macros in higher-level languages gained popularity only after LISP had first been developed, and macros in LISP are a later addition to the language. Any source program, of course, in any programming language, which is internally redundant – that is which contains repeated groups of statements – can be replaced by a shorter program, in which each group of statements which is repeated is given a name; the name, rather than the group of statements, is then repeated, shortening the source program. Sometimes the group of statements will not be exactly repeated, but only approximately so; in this case, we have a macro with parameters which specify the variations to be made. This is the basic idea of the macro, which is applicable to any programming language. For the specific application to LISP, the reader is advised to consult the manual for his own particular LISP system.

Exercises

1 Write a LISP definition of the RECIP function in terms of other known functions.

*2 Write a LISP definition of a function MAXL in terms of other known functions, where MAXL is exactly like MAX except that it has one argument which is a list of numeric atoms instead of several arguments each of which is a numeric atom. Do not use MAX in the definition of MAXL.

3 Write a LISP function APAT such that **(APAT L (QUOTE G))** (or **(APAT L (FUNCTION G))**) applies the function G to every atom in the S-expression of the list L, from front to back.

*4 Write a LISP function CONLAB such that if L is a list of the form **(DEFINE (QUOTE (($f\,d$))))**, where f is a function name and d is a description of the function, then **(CONLAB L)** is a list of the form **(LABEL $f\,d$)**.

5 Write a LISP program which can be compiled, and compile it. Compare the running times of the compiled and uncompiled versions.

*6 Write another LISP program which runs longer than the program of the preceding example, and compile it. By making several timing runs, try to determine relationships between the length of the program, its compilation time, and its execution time in both compiled and uncompiled form.

7 What is the value of **(LOGXOR 9 −5)** in a computer in which a positive integer is converted into its negative by:

(a) changing only the sign bit ('signed magnitude')?
*(b) changing all the bits ('one's complement')?
(c) changing all the bits and then adding 1 ('two's complement')?

8 Write a program in LAP called ADDTHRU, such that if *L* is a list with no sublists whose atoms are all numeric, then **(ADDTHRU L)** is a list like *L* in which every atom has been increased by 1. Try to write ADDTHRU so that it runs as fast as possible; then compare its speed with that of compiled and uncompiled versions of definitions of ADDTHRU in LISP.

9 Find the difference in timing between the functions NCONC and APPEND (which do the same thing) by extensive testing.

10 Most LISP systems have an option which, if used, causes a printout by the system every time it performs a garbage collection. Write a LISP program which creates a list structure which gets larger and larger unendingly (so that the program will ultimately terminate because the system runs out of available space). 'Turn on' the garbage collection messages and watch how garbage collections get more frequent as space becomes increasingly hard to find. Also try to determine how much time a garbage collection actually takes.

11 Write a LISP program which uses property lists in such a way that the program runs faster than it would have if it had been written otherwise. Describe in readable fashion what the program does, what its parameters are, and give timing data.

12 Write a LISP program which uses arrays in such a way that the program runs faster than it would have if it had been written otherwise. Document the program and note any unusual timing considerations brought on by the use of arrays. In particular, describe what happens when the arrays become large.

References

1 *LISP manuals*. The manuals for the most widely used LISP systems currently in use are as follows:

  (a) *General:* McCarthy, J., et al., *LISP 1·5 Programmer's Manual,* 2nd ed., MIT Press, Cambridge, Mass., 1965. (This also describes LISP on the IBM 7094, now generally obsolete.)

  (b) *IBM 360:* Stanford University Computation Center, Campus Facility Users' Manual, Appendix C, *LISP/360 Reference Manual* (sold separately from the rest of the Users' Manual by the Computation Center, Stanford University, Stanford, California).

  (c) *PDP-10*: Manual DEC-T9-MTZD-D, *PDP-10 Timesharing Monitor, Programmer's Reference Manual,* Digital Equipment Corporation, Maynard, Mass.; *LISP 1·6,* Reference Manual No. 90708, Applied Logic Corporation, Princeton, N.J.

  (d) *CDC 6400/6600*: Morris, J. B., and Singleton, D. J., *The University of Texas 6400/6600 LISP 1·5,* Revision II, Computation Center, University of Texas, Austin, Texas, 1968.

2 *MLISP*. This algebraic language which extends the concepts of LISP as studied in this book is described in D. C. Smith, *MLISP,* Memo AIM – 135, Stanford Artificial Intelligence Project, Stanford, California, October 1970. It is distributed by the National Technical Information Service in Springfield, Virginia.

REFERENCES

3 *Other texts.* At this time of writing the only other text which is solely on LISP is Weissman, *LISP 1·5 Primer,* Dickenson Publishing Company, Belmont, Calif., 1967. A good general text on programming, which discusses LISP at length (in Chapter 3), is Wegner, *Programming Languages, Information Structures, and Machine Organization,* McGraw-Hill, 1968.

4 *Historical material.* The paper which reported the first LISP system and set forth the fundamental ideas of LISP for the first time is McCarthy, 'Recursive Functions of Symbolic Expressions and their Computation by Machine', *Communications of the ACM,* 3 (April 1960), pp. 184–195. We shall make no attempt to list the hundreds of research papers on the theory of LISP, special-purpose languages written in LISP, and applications of LISP that have followed.

5 *Reference works.* A general collection of material related to LISP is Berkeley and Bobrow, eds., *The Programming Language LISP: Its Operation and Applications,* Information International, Inc., Cambridge, Mass., 1964.

Answers to starred exercises

Chapter 1

1. (b) (DIFFERENCE (TIMES 2 (SIN A)(SIN A)) 1)
   (d) (QUOTIENT (DIFFERENCE (TIMES B C) (TIMES A D)) (PLUS (TIMES C C) (TIMES D D)))

2. (a) $bcd - efg$
   (c) $-(-(-q))$ or simply $-q$

3. (b) Not an S-expression; has more left than right parentheses.
   (d) Good.

5. (a) (SETQ Y (DIFFERENCE A (DIFFERENCE B (TIMES C D))))

6. (b) (SETQ L (PLUS (SETQ M2 M1) (SETQ N2 N1)))

7. (b) Good (and sets A to the value 17).
   (e) Good (and sets ALPHA to the symbol BETA).
   (g) No good; tries to add 6 to the symbol ALPHA.
   (h) Good (the value of (QUOTE 6) is 6).

8. (a) T (or *T* on certain older LISP systems)
   (d) NIL

10. No (see the last sentence of Section 1.5).

ANSWERS TO STARRED EXERCISES

11 (b) 2
 (d) 5

12 (a) 4; they are (3 6 (7 (4 5) 8)), (7 (4 5) 8), (4 5), and (9 3).
 (c) 4; they are (S (3 5) (7 (9 8))), (3 5), (7 (9 8)), and (9 8).

13 (b) $n_k = 2^k$
 (d) $S(X)$ is X and all subordinates of X

15 (a) (12 9)

16 (b) None (error)
 (d) 18

17 (a) 1
 (c) (SETQ BETA (SIN BETA))

Chapter 2

1 (b) 1
 (e) (F G) (see the discussion of QUOTE in section 1.5)

2 (b) DEFINE(((G (LAMBDA (X Y) (LIST (REMAINDER X Y) (QUOTIENT X Y))))))
 (d) DEFINE(((G (LAMBDA (H I J K L M N) (PLUS H I J K L M N)))))

3 (b) (4 P)

5 It will signal an error. DEFINE takes one argument, which in this case is the list (UPSILON QUOTIENT). This is supposed to be the list of functions to be defined; thus the first function to be defined here would be UPSILON and the second QUOTIENT. Neither of these is in the proper format; a function definition is not an atom, but a list. DEFINE(((UPSILON QUOTIENT))) would work.

6 (a) *A*, *B*, and *C* are bound, while *D* and *E* are free.

THE PROGRAMMER'S INTRODUCTION TO LISP

7 (a) *X*
   (c) 9
   (e) (3) (*not* the atom 3, but the list with the single element 3)
   (g) (3 7 8 1)
   (j) (CDR P)

8 (b) CDDR
   (e) CAADR

9 (a) NIL
   (d) T

10 (b) DEFINE(((G (LAMBDA (L) (ATOM (CAR L))))))
   (d) DEFINE(((G (LAMBDA (L) (GREATERP (CADR L) (CADDDR L))))))

11 (a) (COND ((ATOM L) NIL) (T T))

12 (a) DEFINE(((C57 (LAMBDA (X) (LIST (QUOTE COND) (LIST X 5) (QUOTE (T 7)))))))

14 (a) DEFINE(((FIBON (LAMBDA (N) (COND
       ((EQUAL N 1) 1) ((EQUAL N 2) 1)
       (T (PLUS (FIBON (DIFFERENCE N 1)) (FIBON (DIFFERENCE N 2)))))))))

16 (a) DEFINE(((CDRN (LAMBDA (N L) (COND
       ((ZEROP N) L)
       (T (CDR (CDRN (DIFFERENCE N 1) L))))))))
(Note: The last argument of the COND could just as easily be (T (CDRN (DIFFERENCE N 1) (CDR L))).)

18 DEFINE(((DEPTH (LAMBDA (L) (COND
   ((NULL L) 0)
   ((ATOM L) 0)
   (T (MAX (DEPTH (CDR L)) (PLUS 1 (DEPTH (CAR L))))))))))
Note: We could have omitted ((NULL L)0), since NIL is an atom.

ANSWERS TO STARRED EXERCISES

20 (a) DEFINE(((MEMBERN (LAMBDA (V L) (COND
        ((NULL V) T)
        ((NULL (MEMBER (CAR V) L)) NIL)
        (T (MEMBERN (CDR V) L)))))))

21 (b) DEFINE(((NOSUBS (LAMBDA (L) (AND (ATOM
        (CAR L)) (ATOM (CADR L)) (ATOM (CADDR L)))))))

23 (a) (A B C)
    (c) (NIL A)
    (e) (A B (C D (E)))

24 (b) ((W . NIL) . (X . NIL))
    (d) (V . ((W . NIL) . (X . ((Y . (Z . NIL)) . NIL))))
    (f) (((V . NIL) . (W . (X . NIL))) . (Y . (Z . NIL)))

26 DEFINE(((EQUALL (LAMBDA (L) (COND
        ((NULL (CDR L)) T)
        (T (AND (EQUAL (CAR L) (CADR L)) (EQUALL
        (CDR L)))))))))

27 (a) T
    (c) NIL
    (f) T

Chapter 3

1   (b) Two, *K* and *L*.
    (d) DEFINE((((FACT (LAMBDA (N) (PROG (I J)
        (SETQ I N) (SETQ J 1)
        K (COND ((ZEROP I) (RETURN J)))
        (SETQ J (TIMES J I))
        (SETQ I (DIFFERENCE I 1))
        (GO K))))))

THE PROGRAMMER'S INTRODUCTION TO LISP

3 DEFINE(((IND (LAMBDA (X L) (PROG (M N)
 (SETQ N 0) (SETQ M L)
 K (COND ((NULL M) (RETURN 0)))
 (SETQ N (PLUS N 1))
 (COND ((EQUAL X (CAR M)) (RETURN N)))
 (SETQ M (CDR M))
 (GO K))))))

5 (a) (2 5 6)
 (d) (Hint: The time taken to compute (RS L) in one of the two versions is proportional to the length of the list L; in the other version, it is proportional to the *square* of that length.)

7 (SETQ I (SETQ J (SETQ K 0)))

9 DEFINE((((ANYVOID (LAMBDA (L) (PROG (M P S C)
 (SETQ S (QUOTE (SPADE HEART DIAMOND CLUB)))
 A (COND ((NULL S) (RETURN NIL)))
 (SETQ C (CAR S)) (SETQ S (CDR S)) (SETQ M L)
 B (COND ((NULL M) (RETURN T)))
 (SETQ P (CAR M)) (SETQ M (CDR M))
 (COND ((EQUAL C (CAR P)) (GO A)))
 (GO B))))))

12 DEFINE((((X (LAMBDA (L M) (EQUAL (NPARS L)
 (NPARS M))))
 (NPARS (LAMBDA (L) (PROG (K M) (COND
 ((NULL L) (RETURN 0))
 ((ATOM L) (RETURN 0)))
 (SETQ K 2) (SETQ M L)
 A (SETQ K (PLUS K (NPARS (CAR M))))
 (SETQ M (CDR M))
 (COND ((NULL M) (RETURN K)))
 (GO A))))))

14 A way of doing this using PROG2 is:
 DEFINE((((INDEXMAX (LAMBDA (X) (PROG (Y I M V)
 (SETQ V (CAR X)) (SETQ Y (CDR X))
 (SETQ I 1) (SETQ M 1)

ANSWERS TO STARRED EXERCISES

```
A (COND ((NULL Y) (RETURN M)))
  (SETQ I (PLUS I 1))
  (COND ((GREATERP (CAR Y) V) (PROG2
     (SETQ V (CAR Y)) (SETQ M I))))
  (SETQ Y (CDR Y)) (GO A) )))))
```

15 (a) 5
    (c) 7

16 (d) and (g). (a) will produce an error message when either X or Y is an atom, while (e) will produce an error message (for example) when X is a list of one element.

17 (a) −7
    (c) T

18 (b) 24
    (c) T

19 DEFINE(((A (LAMBDA (X Y) (LIST (QUOTE DEFINE)
    (LIST (QUOTE QUOTE)(LIST (LIST Y X))))))))

21 DEFINE((((NWORDS (LAMBDA NIL (PROG (I X)
```
   (SETQ I 0)
A (SETQ X (READ))
   (COND ((EQUAL X (QUOTE P)) (RETURN I)))
   (SETQ I (PLUS I 1))
   (COND ((ATOM X)(GO A)))
B (SETQ X (CDR X))
   (COND ((NULL X) (GO A)))
   (SETQ I (PLUS I 1))
   (GO B) )))))
```

This is a particularly short version which automatically takes care of the case where there are parentheses in the sentence, that is when one of the values of X is a list.

Chapter 4

2 DEFINE(((MAXL (LAMBDA (L) (PROG (M X V)
  (SETQ X (CAR L)) (SETQ M (CDR L))
  A (COND ((NULL M) (RETURN X)))
  (SETQ V (CAR M))
  (COND ((GREATERP V X) (SETQ X V)))
  (SETQ M (CDR M)) (GO A))))))

4 DEFINE(((CONLAB (LAMBDA (L) (LIST (QUOTE LABEL)
  (CAAAR (CDADR L)) (CADAAR (CDADR L)))))))
(On some LISP systems (CAAADADR L) and (CADAADADR L) may be used.)

6 In particular, one should expect to find that the compilation time increases roughly linearly with the length, except for time taken by garbage collections, whereas the execution time in compiled form should increase roughly with the execution time in uncompiled form.

7 (b) −12.

Index

Actual parameters, 26
ADD function (example), 36–37, 60–61
ADD1, 87
ADD2 function (example), 38–39, 68
Address field (IBM 700 series), 13, 44–45, 94
Addresses of references to a list, 8
Algebraic languages, 1
AND, 40–41
  and PROG2, 73
  evaluation of, 72–73
APPEND, 29, 45–46
Arguments of functions, 22–23, 26
Arithmetic expressions, 2, 3
Arithmetic statement function, analogue in LISP, 26
Arrays, 60, 96–97
  two-dimensional, 63
Assembler (LAP), 92–93
"Assignment statements" (SETQ), 6
  and variable binding, 27
  in programs, 57
ATOM, 30
  used in defining recursive list processing functions, 38
Atoms, 3–4, 5–6
  CAR applied to, 28

Beginning of a list, adding new elements to, 61–62
Binding of variables, 26–27
Blanks, 4–5
Blocks (ALGOL), 70
Bound variables, 26–27

CADDR (etc.), 29
CADR, 29
Call by value, 65

CAR, 28, 43–44
  etymology of, 44–45
  used in defining recursive list processing functions, 36, 38, 39
Card games, programming examples for, 65–67
CDC 6400/6600 LISP, 100
CDR, 28, 43–44
  etymology of, 44–45
  used in defining recursive list processing functions, 36, 38, 39
  used in lieu of advancing a pointer, 60–61
Character strings in LISP, 97
Church, Alonzo, 25
Circular lists, and garbage collection, 94
Commas in LISP, 5
COMPILE, 89
Compiling in LISP, 89–91
Compound statements (ALGOL), 69
Concatenating lists, 29
COND, 31–33
  used in programs, 58, 67, 68
Conditional statements, 31
CONS, 28–29
  and APPEND, 29, 62
  used in constructing lists, 62, 64
Constants, 6
Constructing lists, 61–63
  using MAP functions, 63
Continuation characters, lack of in LISP, 35
Counter used in scanning S-expressions, 4
COUNTFIXFLOAT function (example), 47–48
Counting parentheses correctly, 34, 35, 40, 59

109

THE PROGRAMMER'S INTRODUCTION TO LISP

Declarations, in PROG, 57
Decrement field (IBM 7000 series), 13, 44–45, 94
DEFINE, 22–23, 25, 35
  used at inner levels, 25, 87–88
  used to define more than one function, 23, 40
Definitions of functions, 24–27
Dialects of LISP, viii
DIFFERENCE, 2
Dimensions of recursion, 38
DIVIDE, 9–10
Division (using QUOTIENT and REMAINDER), 2–3
Dot notation, 42–44
Dotted pairs, 43
DOUBLE function (example), 62

Edwards, Daniel, vii
Effect of a function, 63–65, 71–72
Empty list, 15
End of a list, in memory, 43
  adding new elements to, 61–62
ENTIER, 86
EQ, 46, 72–73
EQUAL, 31, 46
Error message
  produced by CAR, 28
  produced by COND, 33
  produced by EQ, 72
  produced by the arithmetic functions, 10, 38
EVAL, 73–74, 88
  used in practising with a LISP system, 15
EVALQUOTE, 75
Evaluation function, 73
Evaluation rule, 71
  recursive definition of, 72
EVENP, 87
Execution, and evaluation, 71
EXPR, 95–96
Expressions, arithmetic, 2, 3
EXPT, 86

F (false), 6
Factorial function (example), 11–12, 33–35, 58–59
False (F or NIL), 6
FEXPR, 95–96
First element of a list (CAR), 28

FIXP, 47
FLOAT, 86
Floating point numbers, 6
FLOATP, 47
FOR (example), 76–77
Formal parameters, 26
Free field format, 35
Free storage, 94
Free variables, 27
FSUBR, 95–96
FUNCTION, 88
Function definitions in programs, 87–89
Functional language, LISP as, vii, 1, 10
Functions, in LISP, 1, 3, 22–27
  defined after they are used, 48
  effect of, 63–65, 71–72
  recursive, 11–12, 33–40, 45–46
  type, 47–48

Garbage collection, 93–95
GENSYM, 77, 87
GO, 58
GREATERP, 31

IBM 360 LISP, 100
IBM 700 series of computers, 12–13, 44–45, 100
Identifiers, 5–6
IF statement, in algebraic languages, 31, 32
Indexing of arrays and lists, 8, 60
Input lines, 13
Input-output (READ, PRINT, and TERPRI), 78–80
Integers, 6
  recursive definition of (ALGOL), 12
Interpreter for LISP, 13

LABEL, 88–89
Labels in programs, 57–58
LAMBDA, 24–25, 88
  and PROG, 57
  nested uses of, 27
  used with subexpressions, 16
Languages, algebraic, 1
  functional, 1
  list processing, 8
  logical, 24
  recursive, 11

110

INDEX

symbolic, 6
LAP, 92
Levels of parentheses, 14
LISP, as a functional language, vii, 1, 10
   as a list processing language, vii, 8, 10
   as a logical language, vii, 24
   as a recursive language, vii, 11
   as a symbolic language, vii, 6
   "assignment statements" in, 6
   blanks in, 4–5
   call by value in, 65
   character strings in, 97
   commas in, 5
   compiling in, 89–91
   constants in, 6
   definitions of functions in, 24–27
   dialects of, viii
   floating point numbers in, 6
   free field format in, 35
   functions in, 1, 3, 22–27
   identifiers in, 5–6
   input-output in, 78–80
   integers in, 6
   lists in, 8–10
   logical operators in, 40–42
   manuals for, 100
   parameters in, 26–27
   programs in, 57–59
   recursive functions in, 33–40
   sublists in, 10–11
   types in, 47, 86
LIST, 9
List notation, as contrasted with dot notation, 44
List of available space, 94
List processing language, LISP as, vii, 8, 10
List processing programs, 59–61
Lists, 8–10
   and S-expressions, 11
   concatenating, 29
   constructing, 61–63
   definition of, 12
   empty, 15
   S-expressions for, 10
   unacceptable as arguments of arithmetic functions, 10
LOGAND, LOGOR, and LOGXOR, 92

Logical language, LISP as, vii, 24
Logical operators, 40–42

Macros, 97
Manuals for LISP (references), 100
MAP functions (MAPCAR, MAPLIST, etc.), 63
Matrices, as lists of lists, 63–64
MAX, 87
McCarthy, John, vii, 100, 101
MEMBER, 39–40
MEMBER2 function (example), 41–42
MIN, 87
MINUS, 2
MLISP, vii, 100
MOREHEARTS program (example), 66–67
MULTIPLY function (example), 37

NCONC, 94
NIL, 6
   as basis for COND test, 33
   as CDR of a one-element list, 28
   pointer to, used to end a list, 43
   signifying an empty list, 15
   test for (NULL), 30–31
   used in AND and OR, 41
   used in defining recursive list processing functions, 36, 38
   used in predicates, 30, 39, 65
NOT, 41
NULL, 30–31, 41
NUMBERP, 47

OPPMAX function (example), 71
OR, 40–42
   evaluation of, 73

Pairs, as arguments of COND, 32
   in memory, 12
   used in dot notation, 43–44
Parameters in LISP, 26–27
Parentheses, care necessary in the use of, 16
   in S-expressions, 4
   preceding or following the function name, 14
   techniques for counting correctly, 34, 35, 40, 59
   to specify empty lists, 15
Parenthesis level, 14

111

PDP-10 LISP, 100
PLUS, 1, 2
Pointers, 12–13, 60–61, 93, 94–95
   and dot notation, 43–44
   to lists, 43
Predicate functions, 30–31
Predicates, 30
   recursive, 39–40
   written as programs, 65–67
PRINT, 79
PROG, 57–59
   used in grouping functions, 69–70
PROG2, 70–71
   and AND, 73
PROGN, 70–71
Program variables, 57
Programs in LISP, 57–59
   evaluation of (using EVAL), 75
   list processing, 59–61
   predicates written as, 65–67
   recursive, 67–68
Property lists, 96

QUOTE, 7, 9
QUOTIENT, 2–3

READ, 78–79
RECIP, 86
Recursion, 11–12
Recursive functions, 11–12, 33–40, 45–46
Recursive language, LISP as, vii, 11
Recursive predicates, 39–40
Recursive programs, 67–68
Relational operators as predicates, 30
REMAINDER, 3
Replace functions, 94
Representation of lists in memory, definition, 44
Reserved words, 5–6
RETURN, 58, 65–66
REVERSE, 62
RPLACA, 94
RPLACD, 94

S-expressions, 3–5
   and lists, 10–11
   blanks in, 4–5
   definition, 4, 12
Searching a list (example), 65–66
Second element of a list (CADR), 29

SET, 7
SETQ, 6, 7
   and binding, 27
   at the top level, 14
   in programs, 57
   used for its value, 71, 72
Side effects, 64–65
SIN, 1
Small lists, as arguments of recursive functions, 36, 40, 45–46
SPADEVOID program (example), 65–66
SPECIAL, 91
SUB1, 87
Subexpressions, 15
Sublists, 10–11
   and recursion, 37–39
Sublists of sublists, 10
SUBR, 95–96
Subtraction (using DIFFERENCE), 2
SUM2 function (example), 48
Supervisor, 75
Symbolic language, LISP as, vii, 6

T (true), 6
   used with COND, 33, 67, 68
T, 8
TERPRI, 78, 80
Third element of a list (CADDR), 29
TIMES, 2
Top level, 14, 75
Transfer, in PROG, 58
True (T), 6
Type functions, 47–48
Types, 47, 86

Unary minus, 2
UNITMATRIX function (example), 63–64
UNSPECIAL, 91

Value, of a function, and its effect, 64–65, 71–72
   of a variable, 6, 27
   of an atom, 7
   of T, F, and NIL, 7–8
Values which are lists, 8–10
Variables, free and bound, 27
   program, 57

ZEROP, 31

Indiana Central College
Library

DATE DUE

SE 18 '75			
Chiu			
JUN 8 '83			
AUG 0 1 1999			
GAYLORD			PRINTED IN U.S.A